GEORGE HILLYARD

THE MAN WHO MOVED

WIMBLEDON

BRUCE TARRAN

FOREWORD BY MARK COX

Matador
9 Priory Business Park
Kibworth Beauchamp
Leicestershire LE8 0RX, UK
Tel: (+44) 116 279 2299
Fax: (+44) 116 279 2277
Email: books@troubador.co.uk
Web: www.troubador.co.uk/matador

ISBN 978 1780885 490

British Library Cataloguing in Publication Data.
A catalogue record for this book is available from the British Library.

Typeset by Troubador Publishing Ltd, Leicester, UK

Matador is an imprint of Troubador Publishing Ltd

To all my pupils, these 26 years

CONTENTS

APPRECIATION:

The story of George Hillyard began for me at Thorpe Satchville with Michael Charles. It is due to him that many of the photos, taken there by Miss Kendal one hundred years ago, are available to see in this book. Thank you again, Michael and wife, Sarah, for your hospitality, kindness and support.

Great thanks to Tim Watt for taking the time to edit my words, not once but twice. If time is the best gift then this is what you gave me.

My gratitude to Mark Cox for kindly writing the foreword to this book. And also for the pleasure he gave us over the years with his exploits on the tennis court – at Wimbledon, in the Davis Cup and elsewhere.

My gratitude to the Wimbledon Library – what a tremendous institution it is! Thank you to Assistant Librarian, Audrey Snell, and Honorary Librarian, Alan Little for sharing their time and knowledge.

Thanks to Glen Lockley and wife Nikki. Nikki is the great-niece of Annie Wiseman, who was first cousin to George Hillyard. They kindly invited me to their home in Doncaster and shared the fruits of their own researches into Hillyard with great generosity.

Thanks to Jon Kilshaw for sharing with me his incredibly thorough research into the origins of West Sussex Golf Club. His information opened up a period of Hillyard's life which would otherwise have been lost to me. Thanks also to West Sussex Club member, Daisy Kane, for her superb photographs of the course.

Thanks to Ben Glass for his help with the photos which most needed it.

Thanks to Andrew Moffat, the current owner of Bramfold in Pulborough for his hospitality in showing me around his home, and explaining its association with the Hillyards.

Thanks to Stella Ellis and Gertie Hallwood for sharing their reminiscences of the Hillyards – these two ladies were the only people I spoke to who knew them in life.

My thanks to John Murray who was an advance scout to Thorpe Satchville.

I had mostly finished this book when I managed to get in touch with Ada Dawnay. Ada's mother was married to Jack Hillyard. For both it was their second marriage. Ada showed me 2 wonderful photograph albums belonging to the Hillyard family, full of early photos which she allowed me to copy. Thanks, Ada – it was hugely appreciated.

Finally, thank you to Leicestershire Lawn Tennis Club for allowing me to include photos and pages from their archives.

FOREWORD BY MARK COX:

*A*nyone who is interested in the early history of Lawn Tennis will be fascinated by this commendable compendium compiled by a good friend of mine, Bruce Tarran.

He introduces us to Commander George Hillyard, a fine athlete who had a significant impact on the game of tennis, not only as a player of consequence, but also an administrator impacting upon British Tennis as Secretary to the hallowed All England Lawn Tennis Club, Wimbledon.

From my point of view my interest in the story is heightened not only because of my own intrigue and compulsion with the game itself, but also because of a Leicester connection. I was born in Leicester and also spent many hours playing tennis at the Leicestershire Lawn Tennis Club on the 'en tout cas' courts akin to George Hillyard. One can sense the history where many of the 'greats' played in the formative years of the game.

Coming back to Bruce. I have known Bruce for many years and admired his coaching skill and his ability to make the game of tennis exciting particularly to youngsters, but I have also enjoyed his enormous enthusiasm for the game in its entirety, particularly his passion for the years gone by. This book illustrates this and has been put together meticulously by someone clearly with an insatiable love of the game. He has given us a treasured collection of unique photos and an invaluable insight in the early years of the game in a very readable fashion.

INTRODUCTION – MICHAEL CHARLES
AND THORPE SATCHVILLE

*I*t is probably safe to say that more Wimbledon champions have played on the Centre Court at Church Road, Wimbledon, than on any other tennis court in England. But which would be the *private* tennis court to hold that record?

There is one in particular. A minimum of 30 Wimbledon champions from all over the world have stood, socialised, and competed on the perfect turf of this garden court. The wider roll call includes the American founder of the Davis Cup, the first American to win a Wimbledon singles title, the first Australian, the first New Zealander, and two separate pairs of brothers, all four of whom were Wimbledon champions. Then there were Olympic champions and US champions, a lady who won the Wimbledon singles title seven times, another who won it six times, and another who won five. And many, many more. They all played tennis on this court.

The Elms, then and now

But where was it? Where *is* it?

The story was lost for half a century, and only uncovered by chance. Back in 1972, one Michael Charles came to live in a village in Leicestershire called Thorpe Satchville. Eleven years later he moved up the road into his current house, The Elms.

Michael knew some of the history of his new home. From 1926 to 1938, it had been owned by Sir George Earle, before he moved further upmarket to nearby Baggrave Hall. Lady Crawford bought the property in 1938 and remained until 1957. She was unmarried, and remembered as a great local benefactress, paying for mains drainage to be installed throughout the village.

Sybil Dawson followed, for ten years, and then from 1967 to 1983 the house belonged to George Rich. It was in 1983 that Michael Charles and his wife Sarah bought the house from Rich's recent widow, Barbara.

The original house had nine bedrooms, with extensive grounds, some stables and outhouses, as well as adjoining fields stretching away into the far distance. In these fields can still be seen the traces of a private nine-hole golf course. When Michael arrived, these fields were no longer part of the property and the stables had been converted to a cottage and kept by Barbara Rich. She also retained an enclosed red shale tennis court with old-fashioned lead lines. For a few years Michael and his family were allowed to play on it, but eventually it was converted into a riding ground for horses.

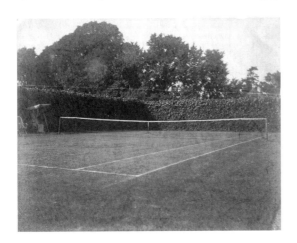 

Left, 'the best grass court in England'
Right, still a nice lawn today

In the summer Michael could use another tennis court – a grass one – in his garden at the side of the house, up against a large hedge. He would mark out the white lines in April with a rickety machine borrowed from a neighbour, and then plant the net posts and attach them to a ragged grey net. His wife and children received tennis lessons on this court from a coach who worked for the Co-op. Sometimes Michael would fit in half an hour for himself after other members of the family had finished.

The court was a good one. Michael had cause to dig down at the edge, and was surprised to find many separate layers of gravel and sand as a base beneath the grass. Clearly someone had taken great care over its construction, though who had built it and when was a mystery.

Two strangers standing outside Michael's front door – the Doherty brothers, the greatest tennis players of their age

On a Saturday afternoon in 1985, Michael discovered the answer. He was mowing the extensive lawn, and therefore not too happy, when a man in a dirty raincoat and trilby hat appeared out of nowhere and advanced across the garden towards him. In his hand was a large brown briefcase. Michael assumed the stranger to be a Jehovah's Witness, and was about to tell him to go away (here, in the telling, Michael lapsed into his own more colourful vernacular). Fortunately the man spoke first, introducing himself as a Mr Kendal, whose great aunt had lived her whole life in another Leicestershire village, Houghton-On-The-Hill. The great aunt was a photographer, who had regularly been asked by the one-time owners of the house to take photos of their tennis parties, and Mr Kendal's briefcase was full of the results. Together, he and Michael Charles repaired to the house to have a look at them. As Michael scanned the black and white prints, and listened to Mr Kendal's story, he began to understand that the history of his house might be a deal more remarkable than he had realised.

The people who had commissioned the photographs were a couple named Hillyard. Each was a champion tennis player of their time. The strangely stilted figures in posed photos, clearly situated around his back garden, were evidently world class (and world famous) sportspeople.

In his garden!

And to think he had been practising his forehand in it only the other day.

INTRODUCING HILLYARD, AND MYSELF

This is the story of Commander George Whiteside Hillyard RN. And being a story of George Hillyard, it is also, of necessity, a story of Lawn Tennis.

First, I should put the man in some context, and for this, I shall introduce myself.

My name is Bruce Tarran and I am a tennis player and a coach. I started collecting various tennis books 25 years ago at roughly the same time as I started coaching. At first these were mainly instructional books which I would hurry through whilst making occasional notes. But I also became interested in old autobiographies. Some names I knew well, and some I knew vaguely. All were great names. Angela Mortimer, Mike Sangster, Jaroslav Drobny, Pancho Gonzales, Margaret Court ... for those who speak the language, they trip off the tennis tongue.

I would extract small memories and relate them to my junior squads as inspirational stories: Hana Mandlikova training in the winter without tennis balls – later using a wooden bat that her father carved, stained red with his blood where he cut himself in the making. This was a favourite. Before too long the pupils learnt to groan when I started upon a new story. But mostly they listened, and even began to quote parts back to me. I thought they were great stories!

I visited the second-hand bookshops in London's Cecil Court, and ploughed through the sport sections, usually finding one or two tennis books to take home. After a while I stopped reading them. This was my collector period, collecting for collecting sake, and rarely reading the books. In retrospect, rather pointless!

I moved to Leicester in 2007 to become Head Coach at the Leicestershire Lawn Tennis Club. This is an 18 court club with 700 members in the leafy Stoneygate area of Leicester. More notably, it was founded in 1878 as Leicester Lawn Tennis Club, one of only a handful in existence at the time. Just a year previously in 1877 The Wimbledon Croquet and Lawn Tennis Club held its first ever tennis tournament with 20 competitors and 200 spectators. If Wimbledon is the mother of lawn tennis, then Leicester is a close relative.

Leicestershire Lawn Tennis Club is old. In the world of tennis, old by any standards. As I began to know the club better, this association renewed an interest in my collection of tennis books. Not so much the modern instructional ones, but rather the vintage reminiscences - the wonderful hardcover books with no dust jackets and rough, creamy paper. Some were formal and crusty; others were lively and irreverent with a subtle sense of humour running through. Reading them was a little like peering at a window into a different age – a window I would love to open.

An unnamed lady about to serve at doubles, around 1904, at the Leicester tournament. The spectators are inside the netting of what is now court 4 at Leicestershire LTC.
I love this picture – one could almost walk onto court and join the crowd, as long as we all had hats!

At first, I was mostly searching for mentions of my new club. Wimbledon had the world's first tennis tournament in 1877. Leicester Tennis Club held its first in 1883, just six years later, and it continued as an annual event, with occasional breaks, for much of the next 50 years. Reading reminiscences of contemporary players and referees I would occasionally come across mentions of The Leicester Tournament.

Another name appeared with remarkable regularity - that of a man who moved to a small village in Leicestershire called Thorpe Satchville in 1896, accompanied by his tennis-playing wife.

George Hillyard. He entered Naval College at the age of 13. At 15 he departed on a three-year, round-the-world voyage serving alongside Princes Albert and George, with whom he enjoyed lifelong friendships.

From the age of 21, on leaving the Navy, Hillyard's accomplishments read like a Victorian Boys Own adventure serial. A top rank international tennis player, competing in tournaments around the world. An outstanding county cricketer. A renowned shot. A top swimmer and oarsman. A champion billiards player. A world-class golfer. An accomplished rider and huntsman. A man who likes to wager, and to win money through his prowess at sports.

His wife is a six times Wimbledon singles champion. Together they bestride the English game for years, winning events across Europe. He writes a book. He presides over successive Wimbledon finals as umpire. He helps found the Lawn Tennis Association, wresting power over the rules and running of the game from The All England Club. At the time his stance is severely criticised by members of the Wimbledon Committee yet, after a few years pass, he is appointed their Secretary in 1907. In this position he oversees the move from Wimbledon's original venue at Worple Road to the current home at Church Road. He helps design the layout of the grounds, and publicly resolves to make the courts the best in the world.

He is an expert on the laying down and upkeep of grass courts. Much of this knowledge stems from the experience gained at his home in Thorpe Satchville, a substantial property on large grounds, containing an almost perfect grass court, a nine-hole golf course and a large billiards room. It also has a red shale court – laid by the famous tennis court constructor, En-Tout-Cas, who, at the time, were no more than a struggling Leicester brick company.

A young Hillyard,
cricket ball in hand

In his position of Club Secretary at Wimbledon he introduces royalty to the game of tennis, escorting The Prince of Wales, later King George V, on the royal family's first visit to the All England Club, in an age when a royal connection was an absolute guarantee of popularity and finance.

He is an Olympic Champion, winning the Gold medal for doubles in 1908, partnering Reggie Doherty. He serves with distinction in the First World War, rising to the rank of Commander RN.

Taken as a whole, the man's achievements were immense. He was an international-class performer at many sports, most notably tennis and cricket. He also had a huge impact in the world of tennis in general that continues to resound today, particularly with regard to Wimbledon.

But equally important, he was a really nice guy, or a thoroughly good chap, as he might have been described at the time. I've read his book, and some other writing by him, as well as personal reminiscences of contemporaries, and I've really come to like him. He wasn't overly pompous, and he was very funny with a rather ironic and dry sense of humour. I would just love to have a chat with George Hillyard, and certainly give him a set or two of tennis. Either on his perfect grass court, or maybe the first shale court manufactured by En Tout Cas – at his home in Thorpe Satchville.

Deprived of such a chance, I'll describe a little of his life. It evokes a different age. When we look at the black and white photos, they appear somewhat antique and distant. But at the time they would have been contemporary, with the grass green and the shale a deep red, and the whites just a little more like cream. Tennis was novel and evolving rapidly. It was a time of life and liveliness – a time like today.

1

FAMILY HISTORY, EARLY LIFE, AND THE NAVY

This is the story of George Hillyard, one of the most important and influential figures the game of lawn tennis has known. And yet almost no-one who plays tennis today has even heard of him. There is no memorial at Wimbledon, no statue at the Lawn Tennis Association, no plaque at the houses he lived in, and his gravestone lies crooked and faded in a Sussex churchyard. It is strange really, how quite minor figures in sporting history can be feted and remembered, whilst others who did so much slip quietly from the record.

This is the life of a remarkable and interesting man. As is normal with such things, I shall start at his beginning.

Commander George *Whiteside* Hillyard was born on 6th February 1864. His father, George *Wright* Hillyard was born 47 years earlier in 1817, with a sister, Louisa, appearing four years later in 1821.

In America they'd be George Junior and George Senior. Much easier! But I'm writing this in England, so from now on will mostly refer to George Wright Hillyard as the father of George, with George himself being the tennis playing hero of our story.

So, to start again, George (our tennis-playing hero) was born in the 27th year of Queen Victoria's reign in 1864. He was an only child. George's father was a police officer in Welwyn, Hertfordshire, when he married Lucy Bird on 24th August 1840. He was 23 years old. Eleven years later he was in Nottingham, working at the County Jail.

On 5th May 1859 George's father was living in Snow Hill, London, when he was awarded the freedom of the City of London. Clearly George Senior was an important man who had contributed something meaningful to his City although I was unable to discover exactly what this was!

By 1861 he had moved to Brentford in West London to take up a position at the Central London District School.

The school was formed in 1849 to serve a number of London's Poor Law Unions, housing children of parents from workhouses and the very poor. Initially it was based in a pauper's school building in Norwood which, after renovation, housed 800 boys. The headmaster of the original school was Frederick Aubin who was paid for every child he took. Aubin wasn't a sympathetic figure – it is said that Dickens based the workhouse master in Oliver Twist upon him. Having sold his school to the London Unions for an impressive £10,000 he was then kept on as Superintendant at a salary of £200 per year. In 1856 a new building to house 1200 boys was constructed in extensive grounds at Hanwell. Mr Aubin moved with the school, and his wife continued as Matron.

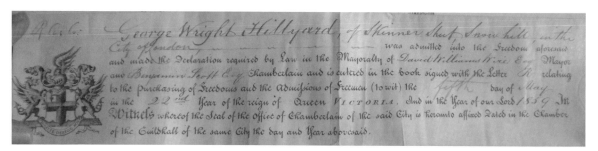

Above is the freedom of the City in the form of a scroll, awarded to: "George Wright Hillyard of Skinner Shut, Snow hill, in the City of London." He was "admitted into the freedom aforesaid and made the declaration required by law in the mayoralty of David Williams Wine Esq Mayor and Benjamin Geoff Esq Chamberlain."
The scroll is dated 5th May 1859. This is two years before George Senior came to the Central London District School. What great service had he done to deserve the freedom of the City of London? I don't know – but still it is an interesting discovery, and a fascinating document.

Aubin died in 1860 and it's doubtful he was mourned by his charges. George Wright Hillyard, then aged 44, arrived at the school in 1861 to become Superintendant. His wife, Lucy, was Matron. Shortly Lucy became ill and a deputy Matron, Mary Mansfield, was taken on at 10 shillings a week.

The institution was at that time plagued by the infectious eye disease ophthalmia which continued to thrive due to the regular turnover of children being sent to the school from the workhouses. A particularly serious outbreak in 1862 affected 686 children, with several of the younger ones losing one or both eyes. It was early in this year that Lucy died. There was a rule that the superintendant and matron had to be married but the Board of Managers were pleased with Hillyard (in comparison with his predecessor, Mr Aubin, perhaps this is not surprising), and he was allowed to stay. The late Mrs Hillyard's deputy, Mary Mansfield, became the new matron.

The marriage had been childless. Before the year was out, in December 1862, Hillyard married again, to the matron, Mary. Their baby was born just 15 months into the marriage. The father was 47 and the mother 37 – late at that time to start a family, and carrying with it some danger. The safe delivery of a healthy son

George Wright Hillyard,
every inch a Victorian
headmaster and patriarch,
in an undated photo.

on 6th February 1864 must have come as a huge relief. The birth was registered on 23rd February in the district of Acton in Middlesex, with the occupation of his father given as 'Gentleman'. On 21st April the boy was baptised George Whiteside Hillyard at St Mary's Church. Given the age of his parents it may have been anticipated, correctly as it turned out, that George would be an only child, and he was given the same first name as his father.

The census of 1871 shows Hillyard Senior still in place as superintendant of the school, with his wife as matron, and two nieces living in – one working as a teacher and the other, Annie Wiseman, a scholar just three years older than the seven-year old George. In the census of that year, George was also noted as a scholar, in the same way as the children of the poor, although his was a more privileged existence. The children of the poor were also labelled 'inmates'.

George later studied at Dr Burney's naval school at Gosport which, at the time, was the best-known in Europe. It was under royal patronage and attracted boys from British and foreign royal houses. Many senior navy and army officers and administrators were amongst the school's 'old boys'.

In 1881 George was in the navy. His father remained superintendant and head teacher. Aunt Louisa was in residence, and Cousin Annie was now deputy matron. Mr and Mrs Hillyard finally retired in 1888 – receiving a pension of £187 and £105 respectively – a generous sum for this time which reflected the appreciation of the Board of Managers.

The Central London District School eventually closed its doors in 1934. The building is now a community centre, although much changed. In 1935 the site of 140 acres was used to house a large building project called the Cuckoo estate. Within this is Hillyard Road, London W7, named after the long-serving headmaster from 50 years before.

A teenage George Hillyard in an undated, posed photograph, standing against a penny farthing bicycle

There was a tradition at the school of inmates leaving to join the navy. One of their most famous residents was Charlie Chaplin whose older brother, Sydney, was sent at the age of 11 to the Royal Navy ship, HMS Exmouth. George Hillyard was only a little older when, in 1877, his father sent him to HMS Britannia to train as an Officer in the Royal Navy. He was 13 years old.

The training of Royal Navy Officers at Dartmouth dates back to 1863 when the wooden hulk of HMS Britannia was moored in the River Dart. With larger intakes of recruits, a ship called the Prince of Wales was put in its place, and was promptly renamed Britannia, establishing a tradition of the name being used for the Naval College. George Hillyard began at this new Britannia on Sunday 15th July 1877 as a cadet. Considering the life that followed, this could be seen as an auspicious date. The first ever Wimbledon tennis tournament began on 9th July 1877. The final was scheduled to be played on Monday 16th July but due to bad weather was postponed until the Thursday. Hillyard began his new naval life at the same time as modern tennis took its first steps on the former croquet lawns of Wimbledon.

Hillyard came from a sporting family and it's likely he knew of the tennis tournament taking place, but he would certainly have been much more interested in the two-day Eton versus Harrow cricket match at Lords on 13th and 14th July. In this he would have felt the same as the tennis players, organisers and spectators at Wimbledon who famously suspended their first ever tournament in order to watch the cricket.

For cadets arriving at such a young age, the naval academy was akin to a good public school where parents paid for tuition. Spending two years at HMS Britannia, George Hillyard completed his period of training on 24th July 1879. He was 15 years old. He was assigned to the HMS Bacchante and made up to Midshipman on 23rd October 1879.

HMS Bacchante.
On which Hillyard and the two Royal Princes, all teenagers, spent three years sailing the world as Midshipmen

Bacchante is the name of a priestess of the Roman God, Bacchus, and for some reason this was also considered a good name for a warship. HMS Bacchante was an ironclad screw-propelled corvette of the Royal Navy, launched in 1876. She was armed with 14 seven-inch muzzle-loading rifled guns and two 64-pounder torpedo carriages, and rated at 4070 tons.

Around this time the two children of the Prince of Wales, and grandchildren of Queen Victoria, were reaching an age for their education to move beyond private tutoring. It was decided that the two young boys would become cadets in the Royal Navy, stationed at HMS Britannia.

Prince Albert was 14 and his younger brother Prince George just 12. There was a wish to keep the two together, even though Prince George was young to leave home. Albert, first in line to the throne, was considered lazier and of weaker character than his younger brother. By keeping the two together it was hoped that George's positive influence over his older brother would continue.

The two Princes served as cadets at Britannia alongside Hillyard. It was then proposed that they would serve on HMS Bacchante and embark on a three year cruise. This was disapproved of, especially by their grandmother, Queen Victoria, who feared that any serious accident on board could leave the kingdom without direct heirs beyond the then Prince of Wales. After much debate, which included the Prime Minister, the Monarch and the royal parents, it was agreed that the two Princes would be allowed to join the Bacchante. The accompanying crew was carefully assembled, and the officers selected with their possible influence on the future King of England born in mind.

Of a crew of 450 officers and men, there were just six naval cadets on board, all appointed Midshipman at the start of the posting in October 1879. Two were the royal Princes – Hillyard was one of the other four. This would have been considered a great honour and he must have impressed during his stay at the Royal Naval academy.

From 1880 to 1882 the Bacchante toured the colonies of the British Empire in the Caribbean, South Africa and Australia, and visited Norfolk, Virginia, as well as South America, the Mediterranean, Egypt, and the Far East. Between Melbourne and Sydney, they claimed a sighting of the Flying Dutchman, the mythical ghost ship.

In his diary, Prince George wrote at the time: *At 4 a.m. the Flying Dutchman crossed our bows. A strange red light as of a phantom ship all aglow, in the midst of which light the masts, spars and sails of a brig 200 yards distant stood out in strong relief as she came up. The lookout man on the forecastle reported her as close to the port bow, where also the officer of the watch from the bridge clearly saw her… 13 persons altogether saw her … At 10.45 a.m. the ordinary seaman who had this morning reported the Flying Dutchman fell from the topmast crosstrees on to the topgallant forecastle and was smashed to atoms.*

Later, with the death of Prince Albert during a flu pandemic in 1891, Prince George became first in line to the throne, and then King George V on the death of his father in 1910. When George V himself died in 1936, a reminiscence of him as a cadet and midshipman was broadcast by then Commander Hillyard.

I was shipmates for five years with our late King, when we were both youngsters. The companionship in one of Her Majesty's gunrooms (the mess for Midshipmen) in those days was of necessity a very close and intimate one. Weeks and weeks at sea, sometimes very monotonous weeks, living on food that was more than monotonous, and also exceedingly nasty. Mostly salt pork and ship's biscuits. Remember, there were no comforts in those days. No such things as electrical freezing plant. So fresh vegetables, fruit and fresh provisions lasted a very, very short time after leaving harbour. Also, one got rather bored at always seeing the same old faces round the same old table, and tempers at times were apt to get a little frayed and irritable. Yet in all those years I never remember Prince George losing his temper. I certainly never had even a cross word with him. Unselfish, kindly, good-tempered, he was an ideal shipmate.

I want you to realize that when he joined up he was only about 12 years old, and when he went to sea, only 14. Yet, even at this early age he had, when in charge of one of the ship's cutters, for instance, to accept full responsibility for the lives of men. He also had to endure all the discomforts and all the hardships which were the inevitable and common lot of anyone who went to sea in those days.

In my humble opinion the training he thus obtained in the Royal Navy, and the strict discipline to which he was subject, were tremendous factors in forming the character of the great and lovable man, and wise king he afterwards became.

It is a description of an old friend, written with affection and honesty. It also tells a little about George Hillyard – he was of a similar age to the Prince at the time described, and dealt with many of the same privations and responsibilities, but without the privileged treatment bought by royal blood. It is the recollection of a fellow sufferer.

2

AFTER THE NAVY, MARRIAGE

Studying black and white photos of this era one can get the impression that everyone in them is prematurely old. With black moustaches, straw hats, striped jackets and fixed expressions, it is difficult to recognise these ancient figures as lively, energetic young men, many of whom were top athletes of their time. Standing alongside them, or sometimes posed in separate small groups, are the equally upright women in their hats and long dresses, hardly an inch of arm or leg showing, staring back at the camera with stern expressions. Somehow a camera lens has turned these groups of young sporting men and women, in their late teens and twenties, into a foreign species.

Of course, in a number of ways this was a time when people really did leap wholly formed from childhood into adulthood. Hillyard went to naval college at 13, and by 15 was a serving at sea as a Midshipman, supervising seamen more than twice his age. When he resigned from the Navy on October 2nd 1885, he was just 21 years old.

Hillyard was in the Royal Navy for eight years, from being a cadet in Dartmouth to his final posting as Sub-Lieutenant on HMS Minotaur. At 21, he was a young man setting out on a new life outside the services. His first sporting passion remained cricket but, possibly due to his courtship, it was mainly tennis that now claimed his attention.

Blanche Bingley was born on 3rd November 1863 at Stanhope Lodge, Greenford in Middlesex. She was the daughter of Charles Bentley Bingley, 'gentleman', formerly proprietor of a tailoring business in Great Marlborough Street, London, and his wife, Elizabeth. Blanche had three older sisters – Emma the eldest by 18 years, Florence and Roselie. By 1881 they were living at a large house in London's fashionable Portland Place. This was a privileged existence, and Blanche grew up surrounded by a retinue of eight servants. These included a footman, a Swiss lady's maid, a French lady's maid, a housekeeper, a parlour maid and a cook.

A wonderful photo from 1900 outside the old club house at Leicester
The groundsman, 'Warrington', knows his place and stands camouflaged at the back, blending in with the foliage

George Hillyard as a young man (about town!)

Blanche Hillyard, famously grim in photographs - this
is one of her more relaxed poses

The Ealing Lawn Tennis & Archery Club was formed in 1882, and Blanche became a member. Remarkably, the Ealing Club would later provide two other early Wimbledon champions in Charlotte Cooper Stery and Dorothea Lambert Chambers. Blanche showed a talent for sport from a young age, and in 1884 competed in the first ever Wimbledon Ladies Singles Championship when only 20 years old. She won two matches before losing to the eventual winner, Maud Watson who, unlike Blanche but along with the majority of ladies at that time, served underarm. Maud went on to receive a silver flower basket for beating her sister, Lilian, in the final. The next year, George Hillyard was still in the Navy, and Blanche spent much of the summer playing tennis. She won a tournament at Acton Vale just a few weeks before reaching the final at Wimbledon, where she again lost to Maud Watson. A Ladies Challenge Cup was presented, bringing the ladies championship into line with the men's, in which every competitor took part in an all-comers event for the right to face the previous year's champion for the title.

Blanche was at the top of her game the following year in 1886. In early June, she reached the final of the West of England Championships, losing to Maud Watson. At Cheltenham, she beat a 14 year old Lottie Dod in the second round, but went on to lose once again to Maud Watson in the semi-final. In mid-June, Blanche won the London tournament at Stamford Bridge, and then Edgbaston with a final against Lilian Watson.

When Wimbledon arrived, Blanche won through to the challenge round, having beaten Lilian Watson in the semi-final of the all comers event. Facing Maud Watson once again, Blanche finally managed to turn the tables on their previous encounters with a convincing 6-3, 6-3 victory. At her third attempt, at the age of 22, Blanche became All England Ladies Champion.

Maud Watson had begun tournament play in 1881 and was considered the best lady player of the age. It was a considerable achievement when Blanche finally overcame her in the 1886 final. In other circumstances, she might have expected her own reign as Wimbledon champion to now begin. That it didn't was due to one of the great sporting prodigies of the time.

The tournament season following Blanche's first Wimbledon victory was dominated by the 15 year old daughter of a wealthy British cotton trader. Lottie Dod had competed in a number of adult tournaments the previous year with some success. In 1887 she came of sporting age.

In tennis terms, the summer of 1887 preceding Wimbledon was a sparse year for Blanche. She won a solitary singles match, as current holder of the London Championships, and besides this played few tournaments. It was no surprise when Blanche was beaten by Lottie Dod in the Wimbledon challenge round – as the holder from the previous year, this was her only match in the tournament. Certainly Dod was a sensation. She had played in her first tournament at just 11 years of age, when she partnered her 18 year old sister and won the consolation event at the Northern Championships. At the age of 14 she beat the then Wimbledon champion, Maud Watson, in a singles, and at 15 went undefeated the entire year, including the 6-2, 6-0, victory against Blanche in the Wimbledon challenge round. Later in her career, Dod played against men, often giving away large handicaps and still coming out on top. She also partnered Herbert Baddeley to a doubles victory against Ernest Renshaw, Wimbledon Singles Champion, and *George Hillyard*. In losing to Dod, Hillyard shared a similar fate to his wife who spent much of her career doing the same thing.

Despite the abilities of Lottie Dod, it is likely their Wimbledon final would have been closer had Blanche not had other things on her mind that summer. George Hillyard left the navy on 2nd October 1885. By 1886 he had met Blanche. This was the year that she spent most of the summer competing in tennis tournaments, including her first victory at Wimbledon. Hillyard was a natural sportsman, and successful at every sport he took part in. It is a mark of his confidence that he now decided take on tennis with every intention of becoming a top player like his bride-to-be. It's doubtful the possibility of failure entered his mind.

By 1887 the two were an engaged couple, and a wedding date was set for 13th July. The Championships that year were from 2nd to 7th July, leaving just six days after the challenge round to prepare for the wedding.

Blanche suffered a great personal loss in the year of her marriage. Her father, Charles Bentley Bingley, died on 20th March less than four months before the planned wedding of his daughter. He ended his life a very wealthy man, leaving a considerable sum for the time of £167, 554 19s 4d. He also left a wife and four children, and a will with seven codicils. Her father's death, along with her planned wedding, meant Blanche played almost no competitive tennis in preparation for the defence of her Wimbledon crown.

As a side-note, the father of George Hillyard - George Wright Hillyard of 2 Park Villas, Church Road, Hanwell, Middlesex - died nine years later on 7th July 1896, leaving a mere £62 7s 10d to his widow, Mary. By the year of his own father's death, George and his wife had moved away from Hertfordshire to their new home in Thorpe Satchville. I remember the first time I visited this house, I assumed that Hillyard had been born into a great deal of money. Maybe his father or mother, or perhaps some rich relative, had left him well-off. I later discovered his father had been Headmaster of the Central London District School – obviously a large public establishment and an important position, but not that of a wealthy Victorian father who could leave a fortune to his only son.

I then speculated about Hillyard's early service in the navy. Could some great fortune have come his way in this short six year period, especially the time spent with the royal Princes? How had Hillyard later managed to finance both his lifestyle at Thorpe Satchville, and his and his wife's globe-trotting amateur tennis career?

It would now seem most likely that it was Blanche Bingley who possessed the fortune, in the form of her father's bequest, which paid for the house and grounds. Hillyard married money, and reaped the benefits.

George married Blanche in Greenford on 13th July 1887, with much of the couple's courting having taken place on the tennis courts of England. George was now playing a reasonable standard himself, and there is no doubt that the couple were tennis fanatics in the most basic (and rather endearing) sense. Just five days after their marriage, the Middlesex Championships began at Chiswick Park on July 18th, and George and the new Mrs Hillyard paired up to win the mixed doubles title. With each, no doubt, wishing to impress the other, the score in the final was a merciless 6-1, 6-0.

Shortly afterwards, from August 1st, the couple travelled to Devon to play in a series of tournaments along the South-West coast. Blanche won the singles at Exmouth against her old rival Maud Watson. In the mixed doubles, the Hillyards reached the final where they lost in three sets. From August 8th they played

From as early as 1880 British players were travelling to Dinard in France to play on their 'sand' courts.
Here a good crowd are watching the local tournament. The sign of the 'Grand Hotel'" can be seen in the background.

at Teignmouth, and then the next week at Torquay. Here Blanche again beat Maud Watson in the final – the last occasion the two were to meet in singles. At the end of August, Blanche won the all-comers singles but lost the challenge round at Eastbourne. George partnered his wife in the mixed doubles, played some other events, and greatly improved his standard of play. On the day of their marriage both George and Blanche were 24 years old. They spent most of the next two months playing tennis.

Did George mind that his wife was more successful than he? Later on, as his own game improved to a high level, I don't think so. But at the start of the marriage, it is more difficult to say. After those early days there was a period when the two partnered each other in tournaments less frequently. Husband and wife pairings often don't work - happy couples off the court can become short-tempered critics on it. This is a fact of tennis life, and so it may have been that the Hillyards decided after 1887 to keep the peace by partnering each other less. Certainly they retained the habit of travelling together to tournaments for as long as they continued to play in them. In the year of their marriage they became one of the most welcome and talked about couples on the British and European tennis circuit. They remained so for many years to come.

As time passed they resumed playing together a little more, particularly at Eastbourne - a favourite tournament. Whatever the realities, Herbert Chipp, a top player of the time, wrote in 1889 of Hillyard: 'In mixed doubles, he and Mrs Hillyard are a much dreaded pair.'

In 1891, George and Blanche had been married four years and were living at Wheathampstead in

Hertfordshire. They shared their home with eight live-in servants, nephews Charles and Clarence, and a new arrival, three month old son, Jack. Wheathampstead was an appropriate town for a lawn tennis player as it was also the home of Lord Cavan, a dedicated enthusiast who had six perfect grass courts in his gardens – more than enough for a large club at the time let alone a private home. Even more convenient was Lord Cavan's excellent indoor court.

Brighton 1898. This is marked as 'Hillyard v Greville', but is clearly a mixed.
George Hillyard and possibly Blanche are this end

An excellent one-page biography in 'Pastime' Magazine, written in 1892 says: *On his day Hillyard is one of the best players in the kingdom, but he occasionally shows very indifferent form. An incorrect decision on the part of an umpire or a few unlucky strokes will often put him altogether off his game, and this too when winning easily.*

This is a common theme in commentaries of Hillyard. It's a reputation that would have made him vulnerable, especially at singles. The biography refers to Hillyard's serve: *Hillyard is fortunate in possessing a splendid 'eye' and a powerful frame. He is said to have a more severe service than any other player and he is often spoken of as 'the champion server'. As, however, the service more often than not consists of two parts – the first and the second – and as Hillyard's second serve is as weak as the first is strong, the title is hardly deserved.*

In other areas the article is kinder: *As a partner in Doubles he has few, if any, superiors, for besides his powerful service he drives very hard, rarely fails to kill a short return or an overhead, and thoroughly understands the tactics of the game. He is as keen as a novice, and usually succeeds in imparting some of his enthusiasm to his partner's play.*

It finishes with some pointers on Hillyard's other activities: *Rowing, swimming and fishing are all favourite pastimes of Hillyard, and he has done well at all of them. He stroked the victorious crew in the officers' race in the Challenge Fleet*

Regatta in 1883, and won the quarter-mile officers' swimming race in the same year at Arosa Bay. In addition to his outdoor accomplishments he is a good musician and an adept with the cue.

Herbert Chipp mentioned Lord Cavan's Wheathampstead court in an assessment of Hillyard written in 1898 – despite the later date I shall include Chipp's sketch here as it does follow on quite nicely from the 'Pastime' biography above:

Of all the lawn tennis players of the present day, G W Hillyard ranks as the best athlete. In cricket he is a prominent member of the Leicestershire County Eleven and has represented the Gentlemen v the Players, he compiles scratch scores at golf, is a capital swimmer, a good oarsman, and no mean handler of the billiard cue. As a lawn tennis player he has stood for several years at the forefront. A man of fine physique and exuberant vitality, he is the keenest of the keen. Indeed his excessive keenness has sometimes led to his undoing. Sometimes his equanimity is temporarily overmastered by 'the flash and outbreak of a fiery mind,' – and then his game suffers.

At his best I know of no player with more commanding style. Admirable length, severity, and good form mark his play. His drive is a very powerful one, hit into the extreme corners of the court at low altitude; he is a brilliant volleyer, whilst his smash is merely another word for a kill. His first service, delivered from the full height of his exceptionally long reach – he stands at 6 feet 2inches – is lion like in its strength; his second effort has more kinship with the lamb. On his day he is a very formidable opponent to the best.

From 1887 Hillyard has gradually worked his way upwards until he now stands on one of the top-most rungs of the ladder of lawn tennis fame.

In covered court play Hillyard is seen at his best. For here he is free from the malign influences of wind, light, background, bad surface, etc, to which he is so keenly susceptible. In Lord Cavan's fine covered court at Wheathampstead he is especially dangerous, and the very best men had to acknowledge him as their master there.

Hillyard is now in the full noon-tide of his career. Probably if he were to think less about the game he would play even better than he does. There might then be no need to look further for the Champion.

Chipp talks about Hillyard's prowess in a range of sports, and the basic strength of his game, but also drops some broad hints about his weaknesses - a soft second serve, and a reputation for being easily distracted. As Chipp said, Hillyard could be susceptible to wind, light, background and bad bounces – quite a list!

Apart from this rather wonderful variety of athletic achievement, these sketches give us a good picture of the man as a tennis player in his prime. Like all top players, he developed his game through many hours of competition, in tournaments, and these will be discussed in more detail later.

3

TENNIS BEGINS

George Hillyard hit his first tennis ball when he was just 10 years old, two years before the inaugural Wimbledon was held at Worple Road. It is likely that his future wife, Blanche, was also introduced to tennis around the same period – certainly she was a competitor in Wimbledon's first ladies singles event in 1884.

Imagine learning to play tennis at the same time as the game itself was being invented. Tactics and technique would be evolving through experimentation and discussion on an almost daily basis. It would be fascinating!

When appreciating the life of George Hillyard it is relevant to understand a little about the times he lived in, especially with regard to the development of what was then the new sport of lawn tennis. When looking back at those early days, some dates can simply seem 'long ago'. Was there really much difference in the way tennis was played in 1878 compared with say 30 years later in 1908? And surely this is all so long ago that it has little relevance to the sport we play today.

In the late 19th century the British moneyed classes were looking for a new game to play on their lawns, as well as in their private clubs. Croquet had proved popular, but was now losing its public, and something fresh was required.

Harry Gem was a solicitor in Birmingham, born in 1819. He and his friend, Augorio Perera, devised a new version of tennis that could be played on a lawn. In 1872 they separately moved to Leamington Spa and, with the help of two local doctors, founded the first lawn tennis club in the world. The court was a different size, and the rules were very different from today, but the founding of an actual members club was a huge step forward. Simultaneously, other Harry Gems were experimenting with racquets and balls in their gardens throughout Great Britain and beyond.

Another influential figure was Major Walter Clopton Wingfield. It was Major Wingfield who introduced a specific game with specific rules, and marketed the result to a wide audience. Memorably he called his game Sphairistike, a possible Greek translation for 'playing ball'. Most participants referred to it as 'Sticky'.

Wingfield was an ex-soldier turned gentleman farmer in need of additional income. To this end he 'invented' the game that was to become lawn tennis by writing a set of rules, laying down (eventually) specific court and net sizes, and providing, in the summer of 1874 the wherewithal to play the game, purchased inside a single box containing four bats, the posts and nets, a quantity of tennis balls, and an instruction manual, all for the cost of five guineas.

Wingfield was excellent at marketing, and he had a winning product. Before long his game of 'Sticky' was being played in country houses across England. Boxed sets also found their way around the globe, to Europe, to India and America, and Wingfield's initial accompanying 8-page rulebook expanded by 1876 to a 48 page fifth edition. There seems no doubt that without Major Wingfield, lawn tennis as we know it would not exist.

But was Major Wingfield's game of 'Sticky,' *itself* tennis as we know it?

A classic photograph from the book 'Fifty Years of Wimbledon' by Wallis Myers. The year is 1883. This is the centre court at Wimbledon, Worple Road, the first international match between England and America. This end are the Renshaw brothers, William and Ernest, who won two exhibition matches against the American brothers – C. M. and J. S. Clark. Note the court markings, the small stand, the smattering of umbrellas and the open feel of the surroundings.

I would say not quite. Wingfield 'invented' a game of tennis for lawns, and then tried to call it something else to obtain a copyright. But he only half-succeeded, and hedged his bets by labelling his box 'The New Patent Game, Sphairistike, *or Lawn Tennis.*'

The rules and scoring were very different, and the courts were a strange shape, wider at the baseline than the net, producing a tapering effect like an hour-glass. It's possible that Wingfield initially intended his court to be rectangular, but in his first book of rules a diagram drawn in perspective seemed to make the court's baseline longer than the net. Wingfield hit upon this as something that would make his own game unique and enable him to preserve his copyright against competing variations.

The net was much higher than today, making the game tactically negative and, in practice, a kind of pat-ball where the only objective was to place the ball back into court over the high net. The service was also very different, the idea being to hit it *deeper*, not shorter, than the service line.

George Hillyard recalled playing 'Sticky' for the first time around 1875, as a 10 year old. He was home from school, and an Uncle had set up a court on the family lawn.

As a first-hand experience of the newly invented game, it is fascinating. In Hillyard's words, his Uncle: *marked out the lawn with a figure shaped like a gigantic hour-glass, with a net across the centre. He told us it was a lawn tennis court. The net was about five feet at the posts and four feet at the centre. There was no net tape, and the posts were thin affairs with little flags on the top, held by guy ropes which were always slipping and needed constant adjustment. The rackets were very small with their heads cast off.*

In this sense, 'cast off' means that the heads of the racquet weren't straight in line with the handle, but designed to veer off crookedly to one side (lopsided in fact).

He continues: *My Uncle appeared to think there were great possibilities in the game, and prophesised a world-wide future for it.*

Hillyard admits to finding this surprising. His Uncle was a retired colonel and one of the best all-round sportsmen in the Indian army. He was a magnificent horseman and shot, and also a keen cricketer - all sports of much greater stature than the newly invented 'lawn tennis'. As a 10 year old Hillyard says: *We youngsters would have none of it. Cricket for us, every time and all the time. Tennis seemed pat-ball, and was pat-ball at that period. Players had small skill, nor was it possible to play anything but a comparatively slow sort of shot, because of the height of the net and the low quality implements. And volleying was unheard of.*

Hillyard took up tennis more seriously around the age of 21, but these were still early days in the development of the game. Ten years on from this childhood experience with his uncle, he regretfully found that tennis was still considered, in the vocabulary of the time, *as fit only for a woman and quite unworthy of a man, and certainly unworthy of a man who played cricket!*

Photos from Hillyard's own album. Tennis tournaments were as much social occasions as sporting events. Middle left is Hillyard's great friend, Mrs Lambert Chambers, posing in front of a full gallery and a smart-looking ball boy.

In fact, as events proved, Hillyard's Uncle was far-sighted. If he visited the Wimbledon tournament in later life, he would have stood amongst the teeming crowds and congratulated himself on his powers of prophesy.

By 1877 there were still many competing versions of lawn tennis. It was in this year that a newly formed tennis club in a small town to the South of London decided to organise a tournament.

The Wimbledon Croquet Club had been formed in 1869 on four acres of land in Worple Road at an annual rent of £50 rising to a £100. Amongst the membership was Henry Jones, who wrote extensively in *The Field* - the most widely read sporting publication of the time - under the name 'Cavendish'. In 1875 he put forward a motion to the committee proposing that a part of the ground be reserved for lawn tennis and badminton. This was accepted, and £25 set aside to make it possible.

Some formidable-looking women, at Hillyard's home in Thorpe Satchville. Here in the middle and on the right, respectively, are Agnes Morton and Dora Boothby. Agnes Morton was twice Wimbledon finalist. Dora Boothby was Wimbledon champion in 1909.
On the left is Miss Vera Spofforth from Australia.

Tennis prospered, and in 1877 Wimbledon became the rather optimistic 'All England Croquet and Lawn Tennis Club'. Along with its new name, the club decided to inaugurate a Lawn Tennis Championship. Mr J. H. Walsh was Honorary Secretary of the club, and also editor of *The Field* magazine. It was Walsh who persuaded the proprietors of *The Field* to provide a silver challenge cup costing 25 guineas to be presented to the tournament champion.

In its first two years as a club, Wimbledon had adopted the laws of tennis as drawn up by a sub-committee of the Marylebone Cricket Club. Across the country there were a host of rival rules used, and it was decided that for their first ever tournament, Wimbledon would produce a definitive set of rules to combine common sense and experience. This job was given to three men – the aforementioned Henry Jones, Julian Marshall, who amongst other accomplishments wrote a book about Real Tennis in 1878 called 'The Annals of Tennis', and C. G. Heathcote, who in 1890 would author the lawn tennis volume of the influential Badminton Library.

The result was a set of rules that has stood the test of time in a quite remarkable way. It is difficult to imagine that anyone could have done a better job than these three friends. They were undoubted tennis visionaries, owed a debt of gratitude by all of us who love to play or watch the modern game.

The original M.C.C. rules were those of a different sport and it easy to understand why a 10 year old Hillyard seemed unimpressed when introduced to the game in 1874. Each player was designated 'Hand-in' or 'Hand-out'. Only Hand-in could serve, or score a point. On losing a point he became Hand-out. The serve was delivered with one foot outside the base line, diagonally over the net and to be hit shorter than the service line. If into the net, the server became Hands out. If over the net but not in the box then it was a fault (so he had another go). In doubles, if in the wrong box, the partner was allowed to hit it. The game was up to fifteen separate points. If the score reached fourteen-all then the score was called deuce, then advantage.

The 'Wimbledon' rules in 1877 changed the scoring system, basing it on Real Tennis, to become much closer to the one we know today. Each set was up to six games, with server and receiver being able to score points. Each game moving through 15-love, 30-love, etc, with deuce and advantages included. Matches were generally best of five sets. Serves that hit the net and bounced in were played as good.

The court dimensions were also different, but this is easier to understand when set against the first 'Wimbledon' dimensions in 1877, and those of today, as shown below:

	MCC 1875	WIMBLEDON 1877	MODERN
Net height at posts (feet)	5	5	3.5
Net height in centre (feet)	4	3.25	3
Width of singles baseline (feet)	30	27	27
Width of court at net (feet)	24	27	27
Net to baseline (feet)	39	39	39
Net to service line (feet)	26	26	21
Weight of ball (ounces)	1.5	1.24 – 1.5	2 – 2.1
Diameter of ball (inches)	2.25	2.25 – 2.6	2.5 – 2.6

In 1878 the net was reduced to 3 feet in the centre, and 4.75 feet at the posts, soon reducing to 3.5 feet at the posts. The service line was moved closer to the net, to 22 feet, then in 1880 to 21 feet (as now). The ball was set at 2 ounces in weight, as today, although this was considered excessive at the time. There have been other 'tweaks', but within a very few years of the first Wimbledon meeting, the rules of tennis were in essence the same as now.

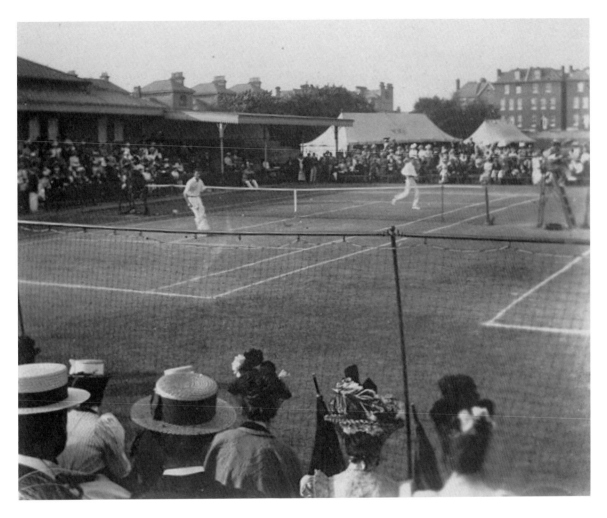

Finals day at Brighton 1898 – Mahoney v Chaytor
Grandstands, umpire's chairs, tents, large crowds – it all has the look of a "mature" sport.
Year 22 in our history of lawn tennis

Considering all of this early evolution, what should be considered as 'Year One' in the life of tennis?

In my opinion, the History of Lawn Tennis, as we know it, was written on the courts of the All England Club at Wimbledon, and it is the adoption of their set of rules which marks out 1877 at the beginning of the game. Of course, if we could go back in time and watch this event there would still be a great deal that would seem strange. But I suppose everything would seem strange, not just the tennis.

Moving pictures and the phonograph were only just invented in 1877 when George Hillyard was a recently enrolled 13 year old cadet on HMS Britannia. There were no electric light bulbs, no private telephones, no

Coca-Cola, no safety matches, no cars, no zippers, no crayons, no aeroplanes, no radios, no teabags, no vacuum cleaners. This was the world he grew up in.

Until 1875 chimneys were still regularly cleaned by forcing young boys to climb up them with brushes. The Victorian attitude to poverty was to place the blame on the poor for their plight; and hunger and extreme hardship was still the lot of a sizeable proportion of England's population. At the end of the 19th century attitudes to poverty were changing - in their own eyes the people of 1877 may have imagined that they were living in an enlightened time, and compared with 50 years previously, they undoubtedly were.

Politically it was the age of Empire. Queen Victoria had been on the throne for forty years and the aristocracy in England were confident of their place in the world. New money was joining old, and the burgeoning upper and middle classes were looking for fresh excitements and pastimes. The Henley Regatta, Royal Ascot, the Lords Varsity Cricket Match – these traditional and iconic British sporting events were about to be joined by a new rival – Lawn Tennis at Wimbledon.

If 1877 was year one, then the Championships of 1900 would be year 24. This gives some feel of context. How would the game have looked, now that it had then been played for 24 years? Would this still be a time of experiment and change, or would it have matured, and be the same as today? Well, this particular 24 year time span undoubtedly saw a sharper rise in standards than any subsequent period. In the first Wimbledon of 1877 the game was completely new. All competitors, including the winner, served underarm at times, and overarm only from the shoulder. The main stroke was a heavy corkscrew slice from the back, or a mad dash and lunge at the net. Topspin was unheard of. But by 1900, Reggie Doherty was winning the singles title for the fourth year running. And Doherty was definitely a 'proper' tennis player, as we would recognise it today.

The first year of the ladies singles at Wimbledon was 1884, so year eight in tennis terms. This is when Blanche Bingley first played at Wimbledon at the age of just 20. In year ten she was Champion. In year 11 (1887) she married George Hillyard, and together they won a mixed doubles title at Chiswick Park. In year 13 (1889), George Hillyard entered his first singles at Wimbledon, winning two matches before losing in the quarterfinals.

The All England Club, with George Hillyard at the helm, moved to its present site on Church Road in 1922. Looking back, it is easy to assume that nothing much happened before this date. Wimbledon at Worple Road may appear an anachronism, a thing of the past, and not important or relevant today.

Can the tennis at Wimbledon, Worple Road, pre-1922 – a period which included the first-class playing career of both George and Blanche Hillyard - be dismissed? Well, 1922 is our year 46, so the period before Church Road was a long one. And these 46 years are a longer span than the time between the opening of Church Road and the year Rod Laver won his first Wimbledon title. Then longer again than the time between Laver's last title, and Federer's incredible five set win against Andy Roddick in 2009. When Church Road opened, the game of tennis already had a rich and varied history. It boasted past champions of originality and genius. It had already established a remarkable sense of *tradition*.

This feeling for tradition can be experienced quite strikingly by reading the literature of the day. Alan Myers summed it up in his book, 'Twenty Years of Lawn Tennis', written in 1921.

Wow – what a wonderful photograph! From around 1905 it features just about every top player of the day and is therefore most likely taken at Worple Road, Wimbledon or possibly Eastbourne. Found in the Hillyard album.

Wimbledon is passing! The Worple Road ground hallowed by the history of the game.

It is rather a tragic thought, this uprooting of a shrine saluted for two score years and more by every disciple of lawn tennis in this country, and from many from distant lands. After another June, or possibly two, dust-stained pedestrians, panting to reach the wicket gate, will cease to jostle each other on the railway footpath; old ladies and young will cease to camp out in that uninspiring strip of unkempt roadway which connects the Worple Road with the gates of the All England Club; waiting motor-cars will no longer convert a quiet and respectable neighbourhood into one great garage.

The reason for the change was simply the popularity of tennis. Worple Road was too small, and it was estimated that each ticket could be sold four times over.

George Hillyard's involvement in tennis spanned this period from start to finish. His wife played in the first ladies event at Wimbledon in 1884. Hillyard played his first tournament just three years later. He was still winning tournaments in 1919, and was Wimbledon Club Secretary up to 1925.

The first year at Church Road was year 46, so 2012 is year 136. The game remains in its infancy!

4

TENNIS TOURNAMENTS,
AND HOW THEY USED TO BE

George and Blanche Hillyard spent much of their time between 1887 and 1914 competing in tennis tournaments.

A tournament in the late 19th and early 20th century was very different from one today. Through the summer there would be a number held across England, both before and after Wimbledon. Almost exclusively these summer tournaments would be played on grass. For the more adventurous there were some additional venues – a May event at the famous Fitzwilliam Club in Dublin, and a growing round of European venues, especially in the South of France and later in Germany.

The English summer tournaments would feature many of the nation's top players competing alongside the locals and host club members. The tournaments were run by club committees, and financial profit was a primary goal with money being raised through competitor entrance fees and by charging spectators at the gate. In an age without television, live sport was an exciting experience and to some extent the type of sport was irrelevant. Spectators often knew little of the rules or etiquette of the game they were paying to watch.

What really drew the paying crowds were 'names,' and in this, at least, little has changed. Top players, especially former or current Wimbledon champions, were much in demand. For a local tennis club to publicise the names of one or two champions would virtually guarantee a good 'gate'. Club committees were known to equip men with sandwich boards to walk around the area, proclaiming the presence of famous competitors.

With grass being the main surface available, it might seem impossible that tournaments were started, let alone completed, if the weather was wet. But the necessity of putting on a show for paying customers meant that rain was sometimes disregarded. Tennis courts themselves were very different, and the pristine grass courts of later years were extremely rare. If not exactly ploughed fields, some tournaments were certainly played on grass that we today would regard as unsuitable for competitive football, let alone competitive tennis. Even a prestigious tennis venue like the Queen's Club in Baron's Court staged football on its grass courts through the winter. Queen's was the home venue for the Corinthians amateur football team, and regular competitive matches took place from 1891 through to 1921. The Oxford versus Cambridge rugby match was also played on the Queen's Club grass. What a job for the groundsman - a few weeks after the football season he would be marking out tennis courts on the same surface! If a tournament needed matches completed, particularly on finals day with many spectators present, then competitors simply performed in the rain, slipping and sliding on the wet courts. They donned metal spiked shoes and did their best to remain standing, with the wet balls barely bouncing on the sodden turf.

Grass court tournament possibly 1914 or 1919

Same tournament – same bare patch on the baseline

In his book 'Fifty years of Wimbledon', Wallis Myers describes the Irish player, Willoughby Hamilton, winning in 1890, and at the same time displays the wonderfully casual attitude to wet weather prevalent at the time – an attitude, incidentally, that George Hillyard took exception to throughout his life: *A wet surface (tarpaulins had been used but the water had run off the sides and infected the balls) helped Hamilton to dispose of Pim as easily as he did; and he was lucky in that his last two sets against Barlow were played in pouring rain, for the Irishman was at his best on a yielding surface.*

Tennis was called an 'amateur' game in the sense that it was 'gentlemanly.' Amateur was another way of saying not working-class. In fact the early winners of Wimbledon and other tournaments took home prizes of monetary value, and often bet on their own (and other people's) matches. A good example of an 'amateur' sportsman of this generation was the cricketer Dr W. G. Grace, who accepted large payments but, as he was a doctor and a gentleman, this was considered acceptable.

At this time, 'professional' *could* refer to someone who made a living out of playing sport, but it also referred to manual labourers, shopkeepers, workers and servants. The cherished Corinthian amateur ethic, which lasted in lawn tennis up to the end of the 1960s, was arguably little more than a method of ensuring that those below a certain social class were not allowed to compete (or more importantly, socialise) with their 'betters'.

Dorothea Lambert Chambers, in tennis gear, outside the house at Thorpe Satchville, the Leicestershire home of George Hillyard This was three years before her marriage so she was still Dorothea Douglas, although already a Wimbledon champion.

Dorothea Lambert Chambers was one of the greatest lady players of all time, winning the Wimbledon singles title in 1903, and then six times more. Most remarkably, in 1919 at the age of 41, she again reached the final, only losing to the shining new superstar, Suzanne Lenglen, 8-10, 6-4, 7-9, having held two match points. Dorothea summed up the origins of many tennis players of her day in a revealing, if unintentional, way in a quote from her book 'Lawn Tennis for Ladies':

Another good way of practising is not to score, but to get some friend to hit or even throw the ball where you want it. I know of one champion of England who always practised in this way. If no friend were available for the purpose, the butler had to devote an hour a day to throwing the ball in the given direction.

One can almost imagine the champion, having won Wimbledon, giving a speech of thanks to the butler!

Winning titles for three years running meant that the (often valuable) silver trophy would become the permanent property of the winner. This was an acceptable goal for the early amateur player. Mrs Chambers again: *I well remember being a set up and five games to one against Miss C.M. Wilson (now Mrs. Luard) one year at Newcastle, when victory for me meant permanent possession of the challenge cup. This cup was very valuable, for it had a splendid list of names inscribed upon it; it had been going for very many years. Miss Wilson seemed so off her game, and I was winning so comfortably, that I could almost see that cup on my sideboard! But it was not to be. (At any rate not that year. I was lucky enough to win the Cup outright in 1908, when it was even more valuable, as Miss Sutton's name had been added.)*

Then again: *I was playing Miss A.N.G. Greene at Eastbourne in 1907; again the Cup would be my own property if I won it. I met Miss Greene in the second round. She won the first set, and was five games to four in the second set, and seven times she only wanted one point to win that match. I was able to make it five games all. It was very bad luck for Miss Greene, as the moral effect, after having had seven chances of winning the match, was so great that it completely put her off her game, and I won that set and the third quite easily.*

What attracted players to particular tournaments? For Wimbledon, it was often prestige and an awareness of competing with the best. For the early Fitzwilliam Tournament in Dublin, it was the famed hospitality shown by the Irish hosts to their guests. For the Devonshire Park tournament at Eastbourne, it was the quantity and quality of the grass courts, as well as an end-of-season holiday flavour aided by the proximity of the beach.

Brighton, Mahoney v Nesbitt 1898. Mahoney won Wimbledon in 1896. So many courts, so many matches

For the tournaments in between it was often a mixture of both hospitality and court quality, but also prizes. Even though this was a time of the supposed amateur, and most of those competing were from the moneyed classes, human nature meant there was always the desire to win attractive prizes. So prizes were offered for first, second and third places - maybe cufflinks or silver medals or inscribed cigarette cases - with their monetary value displayed.

Photos of early tournaments from the Hillyard's own album. So many tents – for gentlemen, for ladies, for referees, for spectators and for tea.

The extent of hospitality would vary from one tournament to another. Costs of travelling to an event might be offered, especially to tournaments abroad. Entry fees could be waived, hotel and food bills quietly met by a grateful committee. Many of the top players had private incomes, others were successful in business - a few genuinely needed the incentives on offer. But when choices of tournaments were being made, players were naturally swayed by the offer of a good hotel, or perhaps the opportunity to win a

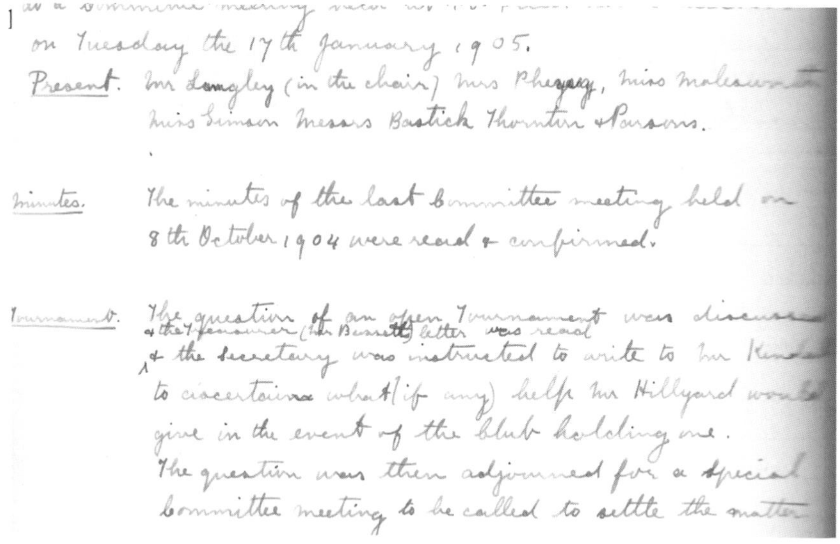

[handwritten committee minutes, partially legible]

> ... on Tuesday the 17th January 1905.
> Present. Mr Longley (in the chair) Mrs Phegary, Miss Molesworth, Miss Simon, Messrs Bastick, Thornton & Parsons.
>
> Minutes. The minutes of the last Committee meeting held on 8th October 1904 were read & confirmed.
>
> Tournament. The question of an open Tournament was discussed & the letter was read & the secretary was instructed to write to Mr Kendal to ascertain what (if any) help Mr Hillyard would give in the event of the club holding one. The question was then adjourned for a special Committee meeting to be called to settle the matter.

> ... the 3rd April 1905 at 5.45 p.m.
>
> Present. Mr Baker (in the chair) Miss Molesworth, Messrs Thornton, Henderson, Bastick, Bassett, Humphries & Parsons
>
> Tournament. The chairman read the correspondence re the insurance against wet weather during the proposed tournament & also a letter from Mrs Hillyard promising her help. The question was discussed whether a tournament should be held. Mr Bastick proposed & Mr Humphries seconded that a tournament be held on the 1st 2nd & 3rd days in June which was unanimously carried

The Leicester Club held its first open tournament in 1883, and these carried on for a few years. On 17th January 1905, after a gap, the committee discussed holding one again.

The committee minute notes: *the question of an open tournament was discussed … and the secretary was instructed to write to Mrs Kendal to ascertain what (if any) help Mr Hillyard would give in the event of the club holding one.*

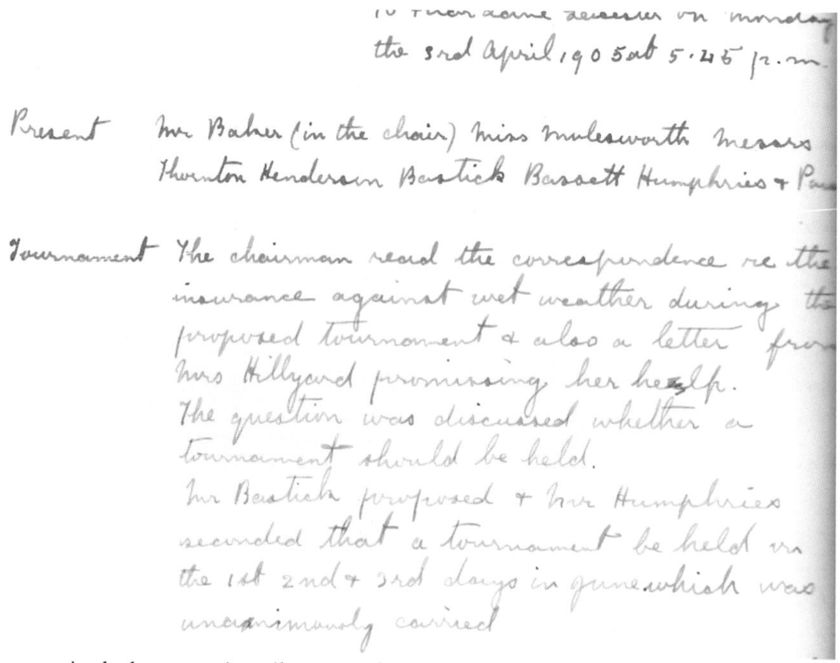

In April 1905 there was another meeting. The minute notes: *The chairman read … a letter from Mrs Hillyard promising her help. The question was discussed whether a tournament should be held. (It) was proposed that a tournament be held on the 1st, 2nd and 3rd in June which was unanimously carried*

This was the start of great days for the Leicester tournament – the close ties to the Hillyards attracting a strong entry and allowing the tournament to carry on, with success, for many years

a particularly attractive silver cup for the third time running.

F. R. Burrow, an early competitor and later referee at Wimbledon, wrote of his first Open tournament in 1883 at Worcester: *I was undeterred by having to pay half-a-guinea (a lot of money at the time) to enter the Open Singles, and half-a-guinea for the Handicap. These fees were the ordinary ones in those days but the prizes were proportionately large.*

Burrow also talks about the Cheltenham Tournament in 1886 when only two pairs competed for the men's doubles for a prize of £27. As he says: *A very nice little sum to depend upon the outcome of a single match.*

Dorothea Lambert Chambers had a different view: *One of the most rooted mistakes in the public mind is that the first-class player is a professional. Many times people have said to me: 'You must be making quite a nice bit of pocket-money from your tennis.'*

'Making?' I say. 'Spending, you mean!' Which always makes them stare in amazement. This fallacy annoys me very much, and is very common. Let me take the opportunity here of pointing out that there are no professional lawn tennis players excepting a few coaches at Queen's Club, and at some clubs abroad; these men, of course, cannot compete in open tournaments.

F.W. Payn, a tournament player himself, in his wonderfully opinionated book 'Tennis Topics and Tactics,' written in 1904 has a chapter titled: 'The Value of Prizes.' He estimates that for competitors who rarely accept hospitality (free hospitality was often offered by wealthy club members during tournaments), the cost per tournament after entry fees, railway tickets, accommodation, etc would be a minimum £10 in Britain, and £15 in Europe. He states that through a small number of seasons, without extravagance but without hospitality, the cost would be six or seven thousand pounds. The value of prizes, if players were successful and accepted hospitality, might, in exceptional circumstances, allow players to break even.

Payn describes, with some indignation, winning three trophies in Europe advertised as £50 and £20 cups. On returning home he took them to be valued and discovered they were worth little more than a pound each. He then describes large tournament entry lists, high entry fees, and restricted levels of prize money. He complains quite bitterly of the unfairness of the low financial value of the prizes on offer to the players when set against the time and effort of winning them. It is clear that financial independence was a pre-requisite for any serious tournament player of the time.

When talking technique, or tactics, Payn places the top British players together in groups of six or seven, invariably mentioning George Hillyard as one of the elite few.

I will mention in passing a remarkable feature of Payn's books. He engages in a vicious vendetta against a contemporary tennis writer, P. A. Vaile (prolific author of 'Modern Lawn Tennis', 'Great Lawn Tennis Players', 'Swerve, or the flight of the ball', 'The strokes and science of lawn tennis', and many more learned tomes of the time). Entire chapters, and many more pages, of Payn's output are given over to a barrage of criticism concerning any opinion ever offered, and every instructional photograph ever taken, by Vaile. It is a hatchet job, and then some, and makes entertaining reading, though, one suspects, not for Vaile!

Another major contrast between early tournaments and those of today was the number of different events the top players entered. At a tournament like Eastbourne, with so many courts and 700 entries, successful competitors might find themselves on court virtually all day from start to end of play. Some would have to scratch from events at the semi-final stage because of the sheer impossibility of competing in so many finals on a solitary day. Almost every competitor who was staying locally, and so there for the duration, entered as many events as possible. First there were level events: the singles, doubles and mixed doubles. Then there were handicap competitions available in matching events. Sometimes there might be additional categories – perhaps a singles plate, a 'mixed' handicap singles for men and women, a family doubles, and so forth. It was not uncommon on the finals day of an English tournament to find a Wimbledon champion winning the level singles and doubles, before battling away in the final of the mixed doubles handicap with a partner who could barely hit a ball over the net.

What a cracking picture. These are the Dohertys, playing at Leicester around 1906. Reggie is closer to the camera, Laurie to his right. The Dohertys won Wimbledon 8 times at doubles, and between them 9 times at singles. They were the best!

Handicap events of this kind have mostly died out, although they remained popular until the 1970s. The system was based on players being given a fixed handicap throughout the tournament, for instance scratch (or zero). If their opponent was +15 then they would have a fifteen love lead in every game. Similarly a player at +15.3 would have a fifteen love lead in three games out of six and thirty-love in the other three. The final decision on handicaps belonged to the Tournament Referee – a thankless task in some ways, although it did occasionally offer scope for financial advantage.

Betting at tournaments was widespread, by spectators, competitors and officials. Burrow talks about wrongly handicapping a player at Eastbourne, saying 'I believe he carried a great deal of money.' Also at Eastbourne in the men's second-class singles handicap final where S. Thol played E. Arrow: *There was quite a big crowd of interested - many of them financially interested! – spectators to watch. And the groans of Thol's backers as he continued to hit smash after smash into the net would have been heartrending if everybody else had not been enjoying it.*

One of the famous early referees, B. C. Evelegh, was extremely proud of the accuracy of his handicapping and his knowledge of form. As a result he was prepared to bet on the results of matches in his own tournaments: *In those far off happy days, players in handicap events who fancied themselves liked to back themselves, and he (Evelegh) never had the slightest hesitation in accommodating them.*

Likewise at the Nottingham Tournament: *One of the difficulties of getting matches onto court on finals day was that everybody backed his fancy for the principal events very freely, with the result that the referee's tent used to get divested of 'helpers' during Saturday afternoon. For the Committee could not resist the temptation of wandering away to the stands overlooking the gallery court, to watch their money flying backwards and forwards over the net.*

Wallis Myers mentions a large sweepstake being run on the outcome of a match in Cannes between legendary Wimbledon champion Laurie Doherty and an American player who was being heavily backed by a visiting countryman. Meeting Doherty before the match, Myers mentioned this to him: *His reply was to hand me ten Louis with the injunction: 'You might get that on for me anonymously.'*

Nevertheless, the Dohertys, whilst clearly enjoying a bet, were said to be the only top-class British players who on principle never accepted hospitality from tournament committees.

In the earliest days, naturally, it was players of real tennis and rackets who were first to try out the new game. Mostly they used deep cut (slice) because they were used to the backboard holding the ball in. But in lawn tennis, with no backboard, slice was less effective, even though the soft and variable balls of the time made killing the ball difficult. It was only when people took up lawn tennis as their first sport that the game became more recognisable as the one we know.

The Renshaw brothers and Herbert Lawford were the first genuine 'lawn tennis players' as opposed to racquets or real tennis players experimenting with the game. Lawford had steely determination and a huge topspin forehand which made him feared from the back of the court. William Renshaw, in particular, had a more all-court game, with the ability to volley.

There were a large number of tournaments held, with varying degrees of success. Wallis Myers stated that one of the most important factors in a tournament's popularity was the quality of local hotels, and this was one reason Eastbourne prospered. He felt the same way about Continental tournaments.

From around 1880 the South of France became a major attraction for British players wanting to play tennis while escaping the British winter. The most popular venue was the Beau Site 'sand' courts at Cannes, but other competitions prospered right along the coast.

Dorothea Lambert Chambers was a close friend of the Hillyards and remembered motoring with them to the Continent: *Touring abroad is both an education and a delight. Monte Carlo, Nice, Cannes, Homburg, Baden-Baden and Dinard, all bring the pleasantest reminiscences. Many of us have travelled about together, which is the jolliest way of doing the tournaments. I remember one most enjoyable trip, when Miss Lowther motored the Hillyards and myself through Germany - an ideal way of 'doing' tournaments! The place at which a meeting is held, its surroundings, also the facilities it offers for amusement in the evening after your day's tennis is over, add to the enjoyment and make a material difference.*

Gambling clubs were an additional attraction in the South of France. This led to a particular scandal in 1921 when it was noticed that large sums of money were disappearing from wallets in coats left lying about

Here are two unique photos from the tennis tournament at Dinard on Côte d'Émeraude of Brittany.
The Dinard Club was founded in 1879 by Englishmen on a piece of land next to the Grand Hotel. The hotel, and sign, can be seen towards the top right hand corner.
Norman Brookes, the famous Australian and first foreigner to win Wimbledon, features in both pictures.
Here Norman Brookes bends low for a half-volley on the clay courts. Both these photos of Dinard are from George Hillyard's personal album.

around the courts during club and championship games. The thefts occurred mostly when the public were not allowed in, so suspicion attached itself to the players. Two French detectives disguised themselves as gardeners and kept watch at the Cannes Tennis Club. They observed the wife of Gordon Lowe, a British Davis Cup player, pick up a coat and remove 5000 Francs from the pocket. When questioned she confessed she had lost money at the casinos and hadn't wished to tell her husband. From the number of times that money went missing, she must have been visiting the tables with some regularity.

Mrs Lowe was sent to court and found guilty but released after two days on 'provisional liberty'. She then quietly (and hurriedly) left the country, her husband having paid off her victims.

Wallis Myers spoke about the Irish player, Wilberforce Eaves (the 'Doctor'), and his experience at Cannes: *Eaves was the cup holder for seven successive years. Nor was he an unsuccessful punter at the tables, having acquired the secret of playing one game late and the other early, and both well. I remember the 'Doctor' once piloting a fair partner through a couple of rounds of the mixed handicap and then, when they came to the third round, on which he had a tempting shade of odds, suggesting tactfully that she should take a seat after returning the service and permit him to win the rally off his own racket. By this happy device both the match and the wagers were secured.*

Myers also refers to: *a celebrated English player for whose modest purse the referee had made special arrangements at one of the big hotels … the English international arrived at dinner ravenous after his sea passage and partook freely of the luscious dishes offered him in rotation. Preening himself on his sound judgement in coming to Dieppe, he was rising from the table when presented by the maitre d' hotel with a large bill for fifty-two francs. The player had been dining a la carte, and at this rate the week would cost him an average two month's wages. Fortunately the referee had the bill paid, and the player went on to win two prizes at the tournament.*

A small but significant number of early tournament players would seek to conceal their identity by appearing under a *nom de guerre*, or *nom de raquette*. This may have been for any of a number of reasons – perhaps a lawyer not wanting his clients to think him less than serious, or a businessman wanting to be away from the office without his superiors knowing, or simple modesty, or often just plain awkwardness. For some reason, the Southampton tournament was particularly susceptible to this and the programme bristled with quote marks, including two winners of the men's singles. Good players as well as bad used nom de raquettes. H. Roper Barrett was a Wimbledon Doubles Champion and long-time favourite who often used pseudonyms in his early career – in Wimbledon of 1900 he was originally in the draw as 'Verne'.

The Irish player and All England Champion, Dr Joshua Pym, was equally fond of playing under a false name. In Germany he was 'Mr J. Wilson,' for some reason, and bizarrely even gave a pseudonym when competing for Great Britain in the Davis Cup against the Unites States in 1903.

The most infamous player with a regular *nom de raquette* was Vere St Leger Goold who competed as 'St Leger.' He was Irish Champion in 1879 and finalist that year in the Wimbledon All-Comers singles, losing to the Reverend John Hartley. Vere Goold faded from tennis circles in 1883 and fell into a life of drink and drugs. He was eventually found guilty, along with his wife, of murder; his female victim's body was found rather inconveniently inside their trunk at a Marseilles railway station.

Because the previous year's champion, P. F. Hadow, had subsequently left the country, if Goold 'St Leger' had beaten Hartley in 1879, he would have had no-one to play in the challenge match and would therefore have been crowned champion. In this event he would undoubtedly have become extremely famous (and featured in popular quiz questions) as the only Wimbledon champion to be convicted of murder!

Talking of quiz questions, Hadow himself has a remarkable claim to fame as the only Wimbledon competitor who never lost a set. Soon after leaving school Hadow went to work on a plantation in Ceylon. He was an all-round sportsman but had never played tennis at all when he returned to England on holiday in 1878. Interested in the new game, he asked a family friend, L. R. Erskine, to show him how to play. Erskine was already a decent player, and the two practiced together diligently, with Hadow improving so quickly that Erskine recommended he enter the Wimbledon tournament that year. Hadow went on to win every match of the all-comers, meeting his teacher Erskine in the final and winning 6-4, 6-4, 6-4. Hadow then beat Spencer Gore to win the Challenge Round, and became Champion without losing a single set. Hadow soon returned to Ceylon, and never played tennis again. The next time he visited Wimbledon was in 1926, at the 50th anniversary celebration on Centre Court, to collect a commemorative medal as a former champion. This anniversary was recalled by Dan Maskell who was a Wimbledon ball boy at the time:

King George and Queen Mary stood on the red carpet stretched across the middle of the court to present a commemorative gold medal to each of the 34 former champions … It was a wonderful sight with all the competitors of the 1926 meeting assembled on court, and Commander Hillyard standing at the front of the Royal Box with his megaphone announcing each champion in turn.

From the earliest days, tournaments waxed and waned. Some took place for a single year, others for a succession of years before disappearing forever. Some would come, then go, then appear again as new committee members were persuaded to run them. Other venues took wing, and became permanent fixtures in the tennis calendar. Not all tournaments were of high quality – some attracted only local players while others were populated by the tennis circus of the travelling elite and commanded huge crowds and increasingly enthusiastic reports in the National Press.

Alongside the British tournaments, those of France and Germany offered adventurous travel to fashionable foreign fields to play tennis on red clay courts beneath a Continental sun.

Hillyard's first tournament was in 1887. His last of note was in 1919. Throughout those pre-war days, tennis tournaments were almost exclusively the home of the young British moneyed elite, with a sprinkling of rich foreigners. They were truly the upper classes at play.

A group of champion competitors at the Newcastle tournament in 1905.
George Hillyard is at the back, pipe in hand, hopefully not dropping ash on the head of his wife who sits in front of him.

THORPE SATCHVILLE

eorge Hillyard played his first cricket match for Leicestershire in 1894. At that time a birth or residential qualification was necessary to represent a county team, which implies that Hillyard was living in Leicestershire from at least 1893. In 1896 the Hillyards moved into the Elms - a large house with extensive grounds in Thorpe Satchville in the district of Melton Mowbray, about 10 miles north-east of the city of Leicester. Thorpe Satchville was then, and remains, a tiny village in the East Midlands. But when contemporaries spoke about 'Thorpe Satchville', or simply 'Thorpe', they were referring to the home of the Hillyards.

To the left is the Hillyard's own nine-hole golf course, the gardener at work on the nearest green.
Right – today only traces remain

Thorpe Satchville was a substantial nine-bedroom property. Most attractive to the Hillyards would have been the large grounds, offering enough space to construct two tennis courts and a nine-hole golf course.

George Hillyard was later to be the driving force behind one the finest golf courses in England, so it seems reasonable to assume he had a hand in creating the one on his own property, but there is no evidence of when or how. Sadly the course itself is no longer in existence, although remains of some holes can still be seen.

As well as playing at his home, Hillyard also competed at The Leicestershire Golf Club and played there regularly. The club's centenary history states: "In 1897, the Easter Meeting was extended to two days, a Bogey competition for a silver cup, presented by the Secretary, being presented by the Secretary. The Bogey competition was won by G W Hillyard with a score of 8 holes up, receiving 3 strokes. He returned a gross score of 80, *which was a new Amateur record for the 18 holes.*"

Presumably, however, his first task would have been the grass tennis court. It is to the left of the house as one faces the front door, less than a hundred yards away. From the side of the house it is fewer than twenty paces.

The court remains surrounded by high hedges on two sides, as recommended in Hillyard's book on the subject. From photographs of the time it would seem there was a mixture of high fencing, hedges and lower wooden fencing on different sides of the court. The feeling is one of an enclosed space, whilst the side facing the house is more open to accommodate spectators.

This court was built early on, but their second court was not constructed until 1905. This was originally laid as an asphalt surface, later changed to shale in 1909. The requirement was to have an all-weather surface when the grass was not in play. This court is situated below the grass court, with each hidden from the other. To reach the hard court from above one walks around to the left, and meanders down a wooded bank. Through the trees an almost invisible path drops down to the side of a fence. When built there may have been easier access, but the court is no longer a part of the property and has sadly been converted to a riding ground for horses. Pictures from the time show an enclosed tennis court completely surrounded by very high chain link fencing with a hedge reaching half-way up.

On the right, Hillyard's first hard asphalt court at Thorpe Satchville, before En-tous-cas built one on top of it. Left is the present day view, now used for riding

The Hillyards added a conservatory in 1899. This was next to the school room built for daughter Marjorie, later the billiards room, and just a few paces from the grass court. It allowed spectators to sit and watch the tennis in comfort and can be seen in photographs from the time. The conservatory no longer exists, but I originally discovered details of its construction through an internet search, finding the date, the name, and more importantly, the address of the house where the Hillyards lived. It was this discovery which enabled me to locate the house, and later to pay a visit.

One of the great pleasures of the Hillyards was to hold house parties at Thorpe Satchville – often large ones - and to invite their tennis friends to play on their courts. John O'Gaunt railway station opened in 1879 and closed in 1953. It offered a short one-mile walk to Thorpe Satchville, and would have been the main artery in and out of the village. When Hillyard went back and forth to Wimbledon, he mostly travelled by train. Wimbledon Champion Tony Wilding wrote in his autobiography in 1912: *Nevertheless the best matches of a private nature I have ever played have been in England at Thorpe Satchville, the delightful home in Leicestershire of Mr and Mrs George Hillyard. - Many a strenuous, evenly balanced contest has been waged here. Perfect conditions, all of us in the mood to play, the match pre-arranged, every attribute tended to bring out the best tennis.*

From 1896 to 1914 just about every strong foreign player who visited Britain, alongside most strong British players, winded up at Thorpe Satchville playing tennis on one or both of Hillyard's two courts. Three local tennis tournaments at Ashby, Leicester and Nottingham, benefitted greatly from their association with the Hillyards. Wimbledon Referee, Frank Burrow writes: *the fine entry which Nottingham invariably received was largely due to the fact that the Hillyards always had a house-party for the meeting, and brought lots of good players with them over from Thorpe Satchville.* He then gives a list of players for 1911 which includes three Wimbledon singles champions and many other top players of the time, the majority of whom would have been guests of the Hillyards and their neighbours.

When the Hillyards won the All England Married Couples Championship Cup at Nottingham in 1912, the committee presented them with: *a fine piece of plate as a silver wedding present, and as a mark of the indebtedness of the tournament to them for being so largely instrumental in getting the best players to come to the meeting.*

Leicester Tennis Club was the venue of the nearest tournament to Thorpe Satchville. The Club retains in its archives the minutes of committee meetings from its earliest days. Amongst them is a copy of a letter sent to members on April 17th 1906, from Honorary Secretaries of the time, Hilda M. Harding and T. D. Newham. It promises that: *Your committee has been actively engaged in preparing for the coming season, and desires to call the attention of Members to the following arrangements that have been made.*

1 - An Open Tournament to be held on June 21st, 22nd and 23rd, in which Mr and Mrs Hillyard and their friends (including Mr H. L. Doherty, Dr Eaves and others) have promised to play.

Leicester Lawn Tennis Club.

DEAR

Your committee has been actively engaged in preparing for the coming season, and desires to call the attention of Members to the following arrangements that have been made :—

1.—An Open Tournament to be held on June 21st, 22nd, and 23rd, in which Mr and Mrs. Hillyard and their friends (including Mr. H. L. Doherty, Dr. Eaves and others) have promised to play.

2.—Four Saturday Afternoon Club Tournaments in addition to the usual Club Championships.

3.—Home and Away Matches, 1st and 2nd Teams, for both ladies and gentlemen.

It is hoped that the above arrangements will prove of interest to all the Members.

Your Committee hopes that you will do your best to secure New Members for the coming season, and the Secretaries will be pleased to receive the names of ladies and gentlemen desiring to join the Club.

Your attention is specially directed to the enclosed notice calling an Extraordinary General Meeting.

The Ground will be opened for play on Saturday, May 5th, weather permitting.

Hon. { HILDA M. HARDING, The Gables, St. Marys Road.
Secs. { T. D. NEWHAM, 38 West Street.

APRIL 17TH, 1906.

The original letter to members sent in April, 1906

Such a letter, confirming the presence of Wimbledon Champions at a tournament, would have guaranteed a good 'gate' and a profit for the host club. It is also interesting what amazing quality and quantity was covered by the phrase 'and others' when mentioning the promises of the Hillyards.

This is explained in the magazine, 'Lawn Tennis and Badminton', dated June 27th 1906, which carries two excellent stories by 'C.A.V.' – one concerning the Leicester tournament mentioned above, and the other a weekend spent at Thorpe Satchville.

The first is particularly gushing about the tournament. In fact this seems to be C.A.V.'s general house style. He gushes with the best!

'The finest and most successful little tournament I have ever been to!' was the universal opinion of every player and spectator who visited the Leicester meeting on Thursday, Friday and Saturday last. During the last decade and more the writer has been to nearly every important meeting at home and abroad, but has never yet taken part in a meeting where the average play has been so high class, the arrangements and management so excellent, and the weather conditions so perfect as they were at Leicester last week.

Photos from the Leicester tournament, around 1906

Lawn Tennis Tournament at Leicester: Some of the players

FRONT ROW (*left to right*): A. W. Gore, Miss May Sutton, Mrs. Hillyard, Miss Morton, Miss Pinckney, Miss Kentish

AT BACK (*right to left*): Mr. R. J. Crawford, Mrs. Crawford, H. L. Doherty, Mr. Davys, Mr. Hillyard, W. V. Eaves, O. Pease, Mr. Ball-Greene, Mr. Wilding, and R. F. Doherty

The Tournament, being a sort of test for the Championship, now in progress, caused much interest, Miss Sutton being an especial attraction

A galaxy of stars! This is a photo in the local paper in 1906. All would have either stayed or played at Thorpe Satchville that week, as well being persuaded to attend the Leicester tournament by Blanche (as a club committee minute shows). You can also put faces to some of the names in the two *Lawn Tennis and Badminton* articles for that week.

Honour to whom honour is due! Let it at once be said that it is to Mr and Mrs G W Hillyard that this charming little meeting – a fitting lever de rideau to the championships – owes all its success. Were it not for the kind hospitality so liberally exercised by the fair chatelaine of Thorpe Satchville, the Leicester Tournament – only established 3 or so years ago - would certainly not lay claim to be now called the finest 3-day meeting in the world.

The Leicester Tournament was actually first held in 1883, but the writer was clearly not aware of this. He continues: *Is it surprising that visitors from all parts of the country hurried to Leicester when they read in the papers of such a galaxy of talent? That the Leicester v Essex cricket match was deserted, and close to 2,000 people were present around the courts on Saturday last? No matter what time of day one stepped onto the ground, some of the 'cracks' were always playing. The two Dohertys, Gore, Riseley, Hillyard, Eaves, Cazalet, Ball-Greene, Wilding, Kreigh Collins, Beamish, Powell, Miss Sutton, Miss Lowther, Mrs Hillyard, Miss Pinckney, Miss Morton, Miss Longhurst, Miss Eastlake – are these not the names of the foremost players in the land, and a list of entries which even Wimbledon would be proud?*

Even allowing for the writer's enthusiasm, this is an incredible list of top players of the time. May Sutton was over from America, about to win Wimbledon. The Doherty brothers were Wimbledon champions and Tony Wilding was about to become one. The Hillyards had collected an impressive group of players for their colleagues on the Leicester tournament committee. No wonder such a crowd turned up (and paid an entrance fee) to watch the final.

In the same issue the same writer, still gushing, describes the final day of his stay at Thorpe Satchville during the Leicester tournament.

Another glorious morning, as we wake up at 7am and peep out of the little window of the cottage at Thorpe Satchville. It had rained heavily overnight and it must have been about 3am when we heard the rain pattering down against the open windows. A most refreshing and much-needed downpour, to be sure.

It had been terribly hot on the Leicester courts on Saturday. What tennis! We lie in bed and recall some of the big matches to our memory. Gore's drives, Riseley's whipping serves, Ball-Greene's tricky drop shots, R.F.'s smashes - rather woody sometimes — but no matter!

Ball-Greene looks in at eight and suggests a stroll down to the Springs and a glass of 'Bessie'. What? We're at Thorpe Satchville, not at Homburg. Yesterday's sun must have affected him. A cup of tea arrives at 8.15 with the news that breakfast will be ready at 9. Jump up, and are down at the house 20 minutes later. What a scene as we stand out front under those big trees and let our eyes wander across the country! That marvellous little 9-hole golf course of Hillyard's is before us. Few players have ever beaten him, nor has anyone equalled his record of 32 on it. Jimmy Braid and Taylor say it is one of the finest in the country.

Ladies at Thorpe Satchville – Miss C Wilson, Miss C Greene, Mrs Hillyard, Miss Eastlake-Smith

Some explanations of the above paragraph – Ball-Greene was the losing finalist from the previous day, 'Bessie' is presumably a variety of stout, beer or cider, and Homburg was the German home of a particularly sociable tennis tournament.

The writer then goes on to describe the day. *They hear the muffled thunder of a motor mower on the lawn tennis court: What a perfect court! A billiard table is not more level, or truer. And what a perfect background of English and Irish ivy! 'See Naples and then die,' people say to tourists. 'See Hillyard's court and then die,' one might say to lawn tennis players.*

The gardener tells them play will be possible in one hour. The guests appear and the breakfast gong sounds punctually at nine. After the food there is golf and tennis. Various mixed and men's doubles matches featuring the top players of the time are played out on the perfect grass court whilst money changes hands in wagers between the spectators.

Lunch is at 1.30. They discuss Californian tennis with May Sutton, and an invitation mixed doubles tournament is agreed for Thorpe Satchville after Wimbledon. Eight men and eight ladies, the best currently in the country. They set upon July 16th as a date, organising a tournament simply for the fun of spending a weekend and playing at Thorpe Satchville.

After lunch more players arrive from an adjoining house party including Laurie Doherty and Doctor Eaves. The combined group then go down to the golf course to run races. Top tennis stars, including Wimbledon champions, men and women, run races in twos and threes, for wagers and for pleasure. To finish, Laurie Doherty races Blanche Hillyard over 100 yards, gives her a 10 yard start, and wins.

Back to the court. More matches are played and the writer describes the bets made on them. Finally, in late afternoon, with tennis still in progress, Reggie Doherty drives back to London in his car, with passengers including Ball-Greene and the writer.

The car is evidently: *a splendid 40 h.p. FIAT – finest car on the market. The motor-clock says 4.10 as we leave Thorpe.* The journey is described – joking about nearly running over a dog, then a policeman. *Ball-Greene's hat flying off, and going back to get it. A trip past the Leicester tennis club, lovely villas on right and left, the groundsman smoking placidly on the corner.* A bumble bee attacks them but luckily they are wearing goggles. They arrive at Northampton at 5.40, and then stop at a quiet spot for a picnic dinner. *Most excellent collation. Cold salmon, salad, viands froides assorties, and plum cake. Drink health of fair chatelaine of Thorpe* (meaning Blanche Hillyard). *Three bottles of Bollinger empty in no time. Leave again at 7.15. Pass white auto shouting 'Hoy, hoy!'*

The writer then describes a rather drunken journey – *car moving along splendidly, frequently do over 50 miles an hour* - before stopping for a fourth bottle of Bollinger and finally arriving at St Pancras at 10.15 where their luggage was waiting.

From today's perspective, this article is very much of its time. But it is also more honest about its subject than most writing in this era. Tennis in 1906 was a sport played, at a high level, almost exclusively by wealthy young men and women. They were healthy, athletic and full of energy. They liked to consume alcohol and have a good time. One of the major attractions was the opportunity to meet the opposite sex, and then to spend extended periods of time with them, unchaperoned, at various venues across the country. It was also later stated by Hillyard's son, Jack, that one of the great pleasures of his parents was to act as matchmakers for their house guests.

The father of Prince George, Hillyard's childhood shipmate, was King Edward VII who succeeded his mother, Queen Victoria, in 1901 and reigned until his death in 1910. Edward spent a great deal of time in

Leicestershire due to the area's renown for horses and hunting, and would have been a neighbour of the Hillyards. The Edwardian era is sometimes artificially extended to cover the whole period from 1901 to the outbreak of war in 1914. It is popularly characterised by the wealthy young upper classes with great energy, sufficient money, little work and unfettered leisure time. There was a tendency to excess, often accompanied by rebellion against the Victorian ideals of their parents. However, even at the end of the Victorian era in the 1880s and 90s, tennis tournaments were considered social as much as sporting occasions. The Fitzwilliam tournament in Dublin was reputedly the most extreme example of this, with competitors dancing the night away, before crawling onto court the following day with heavy heads, only to return to the dance floor for the next night's long entertainment.

Most tennis tournaments featured dances, large quantities of alcohol, house parties, wide-ranging social functions, and sleeping quarters with men and women in close proximity. At a time when attitudes towards sexual promiscuity were becoming ever more relaxed amongst Britain's upper classes, it was no wonder they were popular.

Left: After the 1906 tournament described in this chapter, a report from the club committee saying it gave 'the highest satisfaction'.
Under the heading 'Tournament Souvenir' – In connection with the tournament it was felt that something should be done in recognition of the great help that Mr and Mrs Hillyard had given in procuring such a number of first-class entries and in every way supporting the tournament to the utmost … it was decided that Mr and Mrs Hillyard be asked to accept a souvenir of the tournament in the form of a silver salver engraved with the arms of the club and the words Leicester Lawn Tennis Tournament

Right: The silver salver is presented to Blanche by the Leicester committee
She thanks the club although 'she had not expected or wished for any acknowledgement'

46

Equally, amongst athletic men and women, all sport is enjoyed. Therefore an invitation to Thorpe Satchville would have been prized for the opportunity to play many sports with like-minded people. Tennis, golf, billiards, running, shooting and hunting were all on tap, with gambling considered very much a part of the entertainment.

In 1906, May Sutton was visiting Thorpe Satchville and playing at the Leicester tournament. She had originally arrived in Britain in 1905 when she had won the Wimbledon title, the first foreign player to do so. Hillyard says, referring to May Sutton: *Dark horses at lawn tennis don't, as a rule, do anything to set the Thames on fire. Miss Sutton was an instance to the contrary. Soon after arriving in England she came to stay with us in Leicestershire, with letters of introduction from a former American champion, Miss Marion Jones. Now Miss Jones also stayed with us and played a good deal in England a year or two previously, but although at that time Lady Champion of America, she had impressed us more with her personality than her powers of tennis! So when we heard Miss Sutton was coming we said 'Another of those dark horses, no earthly good I suppose,' and thought no more of it. Miss Sutton arrived. I first saw her at dinner that night — my impression was of a nice-looking, rather short girl, with very broad shoulders, and altogether too powerfully built for speed about the court. On retiring I said to my wife: 'There my dear, I told you so, another dark horse, much too heavy for lawn tennis, nothing to fear from her.'*

The ball boy watches on. To his left is Norman Brookes, May Sutton, and the Hillyards. This could be from 1905 or 1907. In 1905 Brookes was Wimbledon finalist and Sutton champion. In 1907 they were both champions, the first year both titles went abroad. What a wonderful pair of house guests! Behind them is the conservatory, backing on to the school room

The next day Hillyard was proven completely wrong. His guest beat his wife, then Connie Wilson, a strong visiting player. This was just before Wimbledon and the two Dohertys were also staying at Thorpe, along with Clem Cazalet. May Sutton must have felt herself in heaven – only days into her English stay, and she was practising daily with the top players in the world.

Norman Brookes, the Australian champion, was also invited to Thorpe Satchville in 1905 on his first visit to England. It seemed almost obligatory that visiting foreign players would make the pilgrimage up to Leicestershire to play on Hillyard's court, and be inspected for their potential, both as guests and as tennis players. He visited again in 1914 with his wife Mabel during a crowded house party. She found a dining room 'just large enough to take themselves, their guests, and the beagles', and added with some admiration that evidently 'the Chippendale chairs were authentic.'

Seven times Wimbledon champion Dorothea Lambert Chambers, who was a huge fan of Hillyard's grass court, said: *It is marvellous what beneficial effect a good court has on play. I have seen an average player, who had always played on bad courts, put up a really good game the very first time he played on a first-class court—I refer to a well-known private court at Thorpe Satchville, perhaps the best in the country. That player surprised himself and everyone else present.*

The reliance of tournaments like Leicester on drawing top players could lead them into difficult situations. In 1914 four 'cracks' as they were known, presumably invited by the Hillyards, were advertised as playing in the men's doubles event – Brookes and Cleather, and Decugis and Germot. It was then discovered that some or all of the four were unavailable past the first day. There was only one possible answer - the 12 other pairs entered were simply told that the whole event would now be played to a conclusion on the opening day of the tournament! Fortunately for the Committee, the weather held out and the two top pairs played out an exciting final in front of a large crowd.

On October 20th 1914 a long article appeared in *Lawn Tennis and Badminton* magazine, condemning the practice as unsportsmanlike. How could it be possibly be correct, argued the writer, to complete the entire men's doubles event on the opening day of a tournament? Hillyard was a pragmatist. He would have disliked the criticism, but have been pleased that his friends were able to take part. This said, the article appeared three months after the start of the Great War. Perhaps by then the four finalists had other, more important, matters on their minds.

Tennis matches at Thorpe Satchville could even hold a world-wide interest, although only a handful of friends and other competitors might be present to act as spectators. How remarkable that the opening of a new asphalt tennis court in someone's back garden should be big news across the world! Below is an article from *The Star* newspaper in Canterbury, New Zealand, dateline October 1905:

Messrs N. E. Brookes and A. P. Wilding, the colonial tennis players, defeated Messrs Doherty and Hillyard by two sets to love (7-5, 6-2) **in a tournament arranged by Mr and Mrs George Hillyard yesterday at Thorpe Satchville, near Melton Mowbray, to celebrate the opening of their new asphalt tennis court.** *In the Mixed Doubles, the best match played was that in which Mrs Hillyard and Brookes opposed Miss Pinckney and Hillyard. It was not until twenty-four games had been played that the latter pair won the first set. Brookes now came on, and, winning his service each time, secured the second set at 7-5. The next set was close and exciting, the match repeatedly appearing to hang on one stroke. Throughout the whole match Mrs Hillyard played her steady and clever game, giving the opposing man* *no license at the net. Miss Pinckney and her partner played sterling tennis, and thoroughly deserved their win. Brookes and Mrs Hillyard proved too good for Gore and Miss Wilson, this year's winners at Wimbledon, the former eventually winning at -6-4, 6-4. The match between Gore and Miss Wilson and Wilding and Miss Douglass rather unexpectedly resulted in an easy victory for the latter pair by 6-3, 6-2. Wilding played excellently, his forehand drive and overhead work being very deadly. Miss Douglass ably backed him up by her driving from the back of the court. Neither Gore nor Miss Wilson played quite to their usual form, the new conditions apparently not suiting them. Following up this victory, Wilding and Miss Douglas gave a very fine performance against Doherty and Miss Eastlake Smith, beating them in two straight sets (6-0, 6-3). In this match Miss Douglass fairly surpassed herself, and put up one of her very finest games. Doherty showed patches of brilliancy, but his efforts were rather spasmodic.*

Home in Thorpe Satchville was a rustic existence. The Hillyard album is full of pictures of horses and dogs, each one named. The photo below shows sheep shearing. Left is a cute photo of the children on ponies with goats and dogs milling round. Bottom left are the beagles.

Thorpe Satchville lay in famous hunting country. The Hillyards kept horses and bred beagles, and Blanche, in particular, was a fine horsewoman who rode with the hunt for many years. During the winter hunting season this was an area that offered 'sport' six days a week with one or other of the four famous local packs – Quorn, Belvoir (pronounced 'Beaver'), Mr Fernies and Cottesmore. A habit of the visiting Americans was to rent the larger country houses, including stables, from their English owners, and buy in the best horses. Their absentee English hosts would reside elsewhere and gratefully accept the income.

On December 13th 1908, The New York Times ran a story headed 'The pleasures of the fox hunt attract wealthy Americans to England. The sub-heading: 'Attractive Lodges in Leicestershire and the Americans who patronize them.'

It is a long article, detailing the activities of the American moneyed elite whilst hunting in Melton Mowbray. It speaks of many individuals by name, with the addresses they have rented and the numbers of horses they have bought. It is an example of the press assigning status and celebrity to people, and then using this to focus on their private lives.

Blanche's beagles often featured as props in their photos and she was clearly deeply fond of them.
Here the top British player, Wilberforce Eaves, looks rather uncomfortable holding one.
Norman Brookes seems to have got away with it
George Hillyard looks on.

That month, shortly after Hillyard won his Olympic gold medal, Mr Reynard of Long Island had 'taken' Thorpe Satchville for the winter. *To the regret of hunting people generally,* the New York Times reported, *Mr E. S. Reynard of Long Island, early in his first season in the Shire, is laid low as the result of a serious accident sustained whilst following the Duke of Rutland's hounds, his injuries comprising three broken ribs and a fractured collar bone. He took for the winter the house of Mr and Mrs G. W. Hillyard of lawn tennis fame, where he has brought his wife and four children. He got together a tremendous stud of four blood horses, and for those acquainted with his nerve and skill as a member of the Rockaway polo team it will be unnecessary to point out that he was a brave and dashing horseman, well able to maintain his place with the first flighters.*

The paper continues that evidently a similar misfortune overtook Mrs Peabody, *a well known American lady,* who got kicked in the head by a horse – whether her own or someone else's it doesn't say.

The 'celebrities' appear to have been quite happy to have their lives examined and displayed as examples of an attractive and enviable lifestyle. More than a hundred years on, little has changed.

George Hillyard was always a lively correspondent in the press. In 1902, the American Lawn Tennis Magazine had printed brave claims concerning the prowess of the American Doubles pair Davis and Ward on their tour of Britain the previous summer. As mentioned later, the Americans had stayed at Thorpe Satchville during their visit and been beaten twice in practice by Hillyard and his partner, Eaves. Then again at Wimbledon, Hillyard and Eaves barely lost to them in a very close match. In Britain's *Lawn Tennis Magazine*, published on April 23rd 1902, Hillyard therefore sought to set the record straight in a letter from Thorpe Satchville, dated April 4th:

Sir, wrote Hillyard, *I notice in Lawn Tennis this week a cutting from the American Lawn Tennis, stating that Messrs. Davis and Ward have conclusively shown that they can beat any other English pair with the exception of the Dohertys. This may be the case but I confess that I fail to see how they have conclusively proved it. They certainly played very well at Wimbledon, and deserve every credit for the good game they put up; but it must be remembered that they came over here in a year when our Doubles teams were weaker than they have ever been before to my knowledge. Two of our best players were out of it – Mr Nesbit in South Africa, and Mr Cazalet only just returned from Australia, not having had a racket in his hand for a year. Despite Mr Ward's declaration re empty honours, it is in my mind that they should again honour us with a visit this summer; they will find at least one team besides our champions ready and willing to take them on for a modest wager, either in public or in private.*

Thorpe Satchville, of course, was a family home. Marjorie was born there, being five years younger than her brother Jack. Marjorie was mentally handicapped and never married, remaining at home with her parents. Her brother Jack was five when the family moved into Thorpe Satchville, and although much of his childhood and youth were spent away at boarding school and then University, this was where he grew up and where he returned to as his home. Jack was a strong tennis player, whilst never achieving the fame of his parents. He reached the final of the Wimbledon plate in 1924, losing to J. Condon of South Africa. His father, who had won the same event in 1906, and reached the final in 1899, must have taken some pride in this.

Coincidentally, I discovered that Jack won the Romsey Open tennis tournament in Hampshire in 1920, beating Major B. V. Harcourt in the final, 7-5, 10-8. Although possibly of little interest to anyone else, personally I found this fascinating – I was born in Romsey and lived there until I was 18. My parents met each other at one early tennis club in Romsey (the Apsley), and I was champion for a number of years at another. How wonderful to think that Jack Hillyard was there before all of us.

Thorpe Satchville was also the family home during the Great War – it was the place that George and Jack Hillyard returned to when on leave, and wrote to when away on active duty. After the war Blanche, in a habit of the time, had all her son's letters home from the front transcribed into a book.

Jack initially writes from London near the start of the war where he has just received a commission into the Royal Field Artillery. He writes to 'Daddy' and mentions a possible fleet action – his father serving in the navy. He finishes: 'In my mind the war is, to all intents and purposes, over now.'

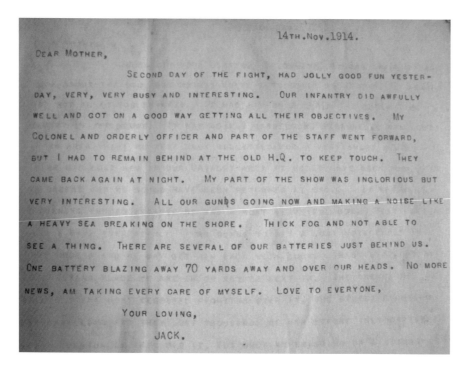

14TH.NOV.1914.

DEAR MOTHER,

SECOND DAY OF THE FIGHT, HAD JOLLY GOOD FUN YESTERDAY, VERY, VERY BUSY AND INTERESTING. OUR INFANTRY DID AWFULLY WELL AND GOT ON A GOOD WAY GETTING ALL THEIR OBJECTIVES. MY COLONEL AND ORDERLY OFFICER AND PART OF THE STAFF WENT FORWARD, BUT I HAD TO REMAIN BEHIND AT THE OLD H.Q. TO KEEP TOUCH. THEY CAME BACK AGAIN AT NIGHT. MY PART OF THE SHOW WAS INGLORIOUS BUT VERY INTERESTING. ALL OUR GUNS GOING NOW AND MAKING A NOISE LIKE A HEAVY SEA BREAKING ON THE SHORE. THICK FOG AND NOT ABLE TO SEE A THING. THERE ARE SEVERAL OF OUR BATTERIES JUST BEHIND US. ONE BATTERY BLAZING AWAY 70 YARDS AWAY AND OVER OUR HEADS. NO MORE NEWS, AM TAKING EVERY CARE OF MYSELF. LOVE TO EVERYONE,

YOUR LOVING,

JACK.

One of Jack's letters home to his mother at Thorpe Satchville, early in the war, in November 1914.

He then serves in France until the end of the war, four years later. The majority of letters are to Blanche with a large minority to his father. There are also a few to sister, Marjorie. The tone of the letters is generally lighter and more positive to his mother, and childlike to his sister. The letters to his father are also mostly positive but contain more grit. There is no doubt that Jack saw much action and on a constant basis. In 1917 he is promoted to Major. Much of the descriptions are of food, clothing and books, sent to him by his mother. He mentions the destruction of British horse cavalry when charging German guns. He often mentions the German shelling and there are occasional more personal passages in which he describes the death of his comrades and the enemy. In October 1918 he sees heavy action but develops diarrhoea and is transferred to an Officer's rest house in Paris where, with a note of heavy pleading, he invites his father to visit and play golf.

In later life Jack gave the time spent at war as one reason for his comparative lack of success at tennis. As an adult he was a man of reputed short temper, who was easily moved to physical anger. It is not possible to know whether his experience of war partly contributed to this but there is no doubt that his letters home are loving, positive, thoughtful and above all brave.

To the left is the postcard of the 'Thorpe Satchville Beagles' that Gertie Hallwood showed me. Above is the back of the card with George Hillyard's initials. Presumably some or all of the beagles were bred by Blanche.

The Hillyard family was part of Leicestershire local life as well as the world tennis scene. Within the village they often rode on an open wooden cart, pulled by a single horse. One of the people I met there was Gertie Hallwood, at 96 years of age the oldest inhabitant in the village. Gertie could remember in her childhood, watching Blanche Hillyard riding down the main road, perched on the cart with some of her beagles. Gertie and the other village children would chase after the cart, accompanied by a pack of yet more beagles running behind.

The jade necklace given to Gertie Hallwood's aunt by Marjorie Hillyard when the family left Thorpe Satchville. Gertie remembers running as a child behind Blanche's cart.

Gertie Hallwood

Ada Dawnay's step-father was Jack – George Hillyard's only son.
Jack spoke lovingly of his parents. Many of the photos in this book are from his original albums, with the kind permission of Ada.

Gertie is a fascinating character who was once the cook at Thorpe Satchville Hall – the largest property in the village. Gertie's family knew the Hillyards well, and she showed me a postcard of the Thorpe Satchville Beagles gathered during a meet of the pack. On its back were the words 'early 1900s' and the initials GH in the distinctive handwriting of George Hillyard, unrecognised as such by Gertie until that moment. She also showed me a handsome green jade necklace which had been given to her Auntie Frances Underwood by Marjorie Hillyard, the daughter of George and Blanche. This had been a present on their leaving the village – Marjorie would have been around 20 years of age, as was Gertie's aunt.

In total George Hillyard lived in Thorpe for close to 30 years. Undoubtedly it was the most important residence in his adult life – a home in which a child was born, children grew into adulthood, and he and his wife moved from relative youth into late middle age. But rather than simply a home, it was also, in the words of one guest, 'more like visiting an uninhibited sporting institution than a house.' One can imagine that to George Hillyard, this would have been seen as the greatest compliment of all.

A rare photograph which shows the whole family together. Marjorie stands at the back, between her mother and Miss H. Lane. Jack is wedged between the men at the front, and the ladies at the back. The men flanking Hillyard look facially quite similar to him, and each other. If they are family, I don't know what their relationship might be.

6

GEORGE HILLYARD IN TOURNAMENTS

George Hillyard loved tennis, and competition. He entered his first open tournament in 1887 at the age of 23 and it was 32 years later in 1919 that he won his last open title in the mixed doubles at Leicester. Hillyard was a man of many gifts, but at heart he considered himself a sportsman, and a first-class lawn tennis player. Any remembrance of his life should include a record of his matches.

A bare list of results may not provide enthralling reading. On the other hand, it is important to record achievements and battles that would otherwise be forgotten. All who play sport have such battles - these belong to Hillyard, and I believe they have great value. A complete record will help to demonstrate how dedicated he was to his sport, how many top players of the day he competed against, how many venues he visited, and how long he remained competitive.

Clearly some knowledge of his opponents would be helpful – what would it mean that Hillyard beat Harold Mahoney if the reader doesn't know who Mahoney was? Or Wilding, or Renshaw? I have therefore penned sketches of a handful of Hillyard's opponents, and mixed these in with the results (as well as some excellent photos!) Hopefully this will add to the interest, as well as giving the results more context. They may have worn different clothes and used wooden racquets, but these players were great characters and world-class sportsmen of their time.

As mentioned earlier, the first public act of the Hillyards as man and wife was to win the Mixed Doubles Championship at Chiswick Park in 1887. Earlier that year Blanche had defended her title at the London Athletic Club by winning the solitary match of the Challenge Round. In the same tournament, George Hillyard entered the singles handicap but conceded a walkover and didn't play.

After Chiswick, the newlyweds entered tournaments at Exmouth, Teignmouth, Torquay, and Eastbourne.

At Exmouth they played together in the mixed and lost in the final. Hillyard lost his first match in the men's doubles but creditably reached the final of the handicap singles. At Teignmouth he and partner J. R. Deykin won the men's doubles to record his first open men's doubles title. He also reached the semis of the singles handicap, and with Blanche lost in the semis of the mixed. He entered the open singles event, but on finding himself two sets down retired from the match.

He partnered E. W. Lewis at Torquay, and won the men's doubles. Lewis was a first-rank player of the time, so the surprise isn't so much in the result rather that a newcomer like Hillyard was chosen by Lewis as a partner. But Hillyard always did have a 'face that fitted,' and in so many social situations throughout his life he simply rose to the occasion and was welcomed as an equal. Of course in the tennis world, although a relative novice, he had the added cachet of being newly married to a Ladies Singles Champion. However, this didn't stop Lewis and his partner, Maud Watson, trouncing the Hillyards in the first round.

George Hillyard in competition. The ball has flown past him and can be made out above the trees as he watches it intently. Out or in, we will never know!

George partnered Blanche again but lost in the third round at Eastbourne. He entered the men's singles and finally won a match, against a Mr W. Mellersh.

A singles contest of note came the following May at the Irish Championships in Dublin. This was a tussle with one of the greatest players of the age – Joshua Pim - who later won the Wimbledon singles title in 1893 and 1894. Pim won in 4 sets, with Hillyard taking the 3rd set 6-3.

Also at the Irish Championships Hillyard lost in the first round in both the men's doubles and the mixed with Blanche. Having gone out first match in every event he might have left Dublin disappointed, but a favourite local event was 'The Fitzwilliam Purse' – a singles competition for those who had lost in the first round. Hillyard reached the final, battling through to meet local Fitzwilliam club member, T. P. Campion, before losing 6-3, 6-1, 7-5. All events had their prizes advertised in monetary value, both on entry forms and notices of results. The Fitzwilliam Purse was advertised as 'one prize of £5', meaning Hillyard returned to England empty handed.

During the rest of the 1888 season, he beat W. Milne and C. Ross in successive rounds at Exmouth (considered good wins), and won the doubles with Lewis against Ernest Renshaw and C. Lacy Sweet. Further matches at Bath, Cheltenham and the Northern Championships gave him tournament practice without great success. Notably, this was the year he first entered Wimbledon, in the doubles, with a Mr William Taylor as partner, losing the first round 4-6, 2-6, 5-7 to Campion and Grove.

Two scenes from tournaments at the turn of the century, from the Hillyard album.
The crowds on the left are so large that this must be a major tournament. The umbrellas are up but play continues.

In 1889 he contested his first Wimbledon singles, winning two rounds before losing in the quarters of the all-comers to Harry Barlow in straight sets. Throughout Hillyard's singles career every Wimbledon competitor played in an all-comers knock-out event with the winner facing the previous year's champion in a challenge round. A Wimbledon singles or doubles champion only needed to win one match to retain the title. This year Hillyard and his partner Ernest Lewis got within just one set of becoming champions - a superb achievement in only his second year in the event. In the semis of the all-comers they had beaten the Baddeleys, and in the final Arthur Gore and G. Mewburn. The challenge round was against the Renshaws and the match went the full distance, before the latter won 6-4, 6-4, 3-6, 0-6, 6-1.

Hillyard's best performance in singles that year was at Cheltenham, where he won the challenge cup, defeating J. Baldwin in the final. Earlier, at the Irish Championships, he partnered Lewis to beat the Renshaw brothers in the semi-finals. The pair then won the all-comers final and following this, the challenge round against the previous year's winners, W. J. Hamilton and T. S. Campion.

Having found a new partner in Miss Steadman, Hillyard lost in the first round in Dublin to his wife. He also went out at the same stage of the singles to Harold Mahoney in a topsy-turvy five-setter. This was a good score against a top Irish player of the time who was to go on to win Wimbledon six years later.

Mahoney had a reputation for a casual approach and was often late for matches. Even in the most important of meetings he would frequently play in borrowed clothes and became known as 'Odd Socks Mahoney.' He had a reputation as a favourite with the ladies, and also a penchant for entering tournaments under pseudonyms which were duly printed in the tournament programmes, one example being 'N. O. Good.'

George Hillyard forged a close friendship with Mahoney and described him fondly in his autobiography:

Harold Mahoney. What memories are associated with that ill-fated player! How many stories are woven around his name! Surely the most generous-hearted, casual, irresponsible seventy-five inches of bone and muscle that ever walked onto a court. Mahoney was the optimist of the lawn tennis world. Nothing daunted his lion-hearted spirit. His great weakness was his forehand drive, or rather it's complete absence. A splendid all-round player in every other respect he could not, and never did, acquire the right method of hitting the ball on the forehand. 'Now George, I've been watching Smith and I've got his forehand exactly. I'm going to beat him this afternoon.' Well, I did wait and see, and it was the same old Mahoney forehand with a lot of cut on it and without the foggiest resemblance to Smith's famous stroke. And Harold would be beaten once again (he never could play Smith). But not one jot did such a trifle abate his confidence. The next time he played Smith he was just as certain he was going to win. What a glorious disposition to have! And what an asset! Of such stuff are heroes made!

Having trashed Mahoney's forehand, Hillyard then went on to praise everything else: *If Mahoney's forehand was weak, his backhand was the reverse and few finer have ever been seen. His great strength lay in his volleying of which he was the master, and as he simply lived at the net, had an enormous reach and a magnificent service; it is easy to understand how he won his many victories. Of his numerous good qualities not the least was the trouble he would take, and the hours he would spend, coaching any young player who showed a keenness and aptitude for the game.*

No more good natured player ever held a racquet, and rag him as you would, in all the years I knew him, I never once saw him the slightest bit out of temper.

He concludes his description with a story about Mahoney, the Doherty brothers and himself playing a golf four-ball. Mahoney hit his shot into a deep and muddy ditch and was trying to play it out when a large horse rushed up to attack a cow and then trampled Mahoney's clubs that he'd left out in the open. It's a well-told story and presumably took place on the course at his Thorpe Satchville home. What I like about many of his descriptions of his friends is the mix of warm affection and gentle humour. He was a man who took deep pleasure in his friendships.

Hillyard managed another famous doubles victory over the Renshaws later in the season at the Northern Championship, this time partnering Mahoney. Hillyard had earlier lost to him in the semis of the singles, and Mahoney was barely off court from a long and tiring defeat in the final when he had to go back on in the doubles.

Harold Mahoney, the taller of the two, in 1898, looking likely to bump into his opponent

The 'Irish Times' reported: *The sensation of the day was in the Gentlemen's Doubles Championship between the brothers Ernest and William Renshaw, and George Hillyard and Harold Mahoney of Dublin. Though the latter had just come off court after the Singles he was soon seen to be in grand form.*

The Renshaws certainly started well, and the remark went round the ropes – 'Oh, the Renshaws will win easily' – and this seemed a good prophecy when the Renshaws were 6 to 2. In the next set, however, Mahoney and Hillyard improved, and the Renshaws went back, with the result that the set went to Mahoney and Hillyard, 7 to 5, whilst the next set was a victory for the same side, 6-2.

The fourth set was the most exciting of the lot, and when Hillyard and Mahoney were 3 to 0 and later 5 to 2, the expected defeat of the Renshaws was discussed on all hands.

The champions, however, won four games in succession, though thrice over their opponents should have won, as on one occasion

the Renshaws were love-40, but still they won. On another occasion Hillyard and his partner were 'vantage when the Chiswick player [Hillyard] wanted one stroke, and he put an easy backhander in the net, whilst the third lost opportunity was when a ball which would have won the game fell on the baseline and was declared out.

At last 6-all was called, and Hillyard and Mahoney getting the next two games, the finishing stroke being a smash, the Renshaws were defeated by three sets to one.

The final score was 2-6, 7-5, 6-2, 8-6 to Mahoney and Hillyard. Harold Mahoney was only 22, Hillyard 25.

Considering the Renshaw brothers had that year won the Wimbledon doubles for the seventh (and final) time, these two wins against them in 1889, in addition to the five-set loss in the Wimbledon challenge final, were notable achievements.

Willie and Ernest Renshaw were the first 'great' tennis players. Hillyard writes:

Lawn Tennis players owe the Renshaw brothers a huge debt of gratitude. It was their genius that originated the modern game. They shortened the childhood period (of tennis) and hastened its growth to its current lusty manhood. May their names live long in the land, and be reverenced by generations of lawn tennis players yet unborn.

The earliest lawn tennis players were inevitably converts from other games, particularly racquet sports. For the Renshaws, lawn tennis was their first sporting love. Once discovered it became their lives.

Hillyard continues: *The style of both brothers was as near perfection as one is likely to see in this imperfect world. Willie was all fire and dash, Ernest more restrained and patient.*

Quite a well-known picture of Ernest Renshaw – but this one is copied directly from Hillyard's own photograph album.

Of the two famous brothers it was Ernest who was George's especial friend.

As Hillyard said "May their names live long in the land, and be reverenced by generations of lawn tennis players yet unborn." As one of those lawn tennis players, unborn at the time, I am certainly happy to do so!

Willie Renshaw first won the Wimbledon singles title in its fifth year, 1881. He held the title for six years running, then again in 1889 after a two year gap. He was fast, aggressive, and liked to take the ball early, generally on the rise, to give his opponent less time. It's interesting that coaches at the time of Agassi liked to talk about 'the modern game' of moving up the court to attack the ball on the rise (I was one of them!). But from contemporary descriptions of Willie Renshaw he was using this tactic in 1881.

Brother Ernest Renshaw played a different game, relying on consistency allied to quick footwork. He won Wimbledon only once, in 1888. Hillyard confirmed that one reason for this was the Renshaws hated playing each other, and so on the few occasions they did Ernest refused to try.

The Renshaws were the first box-office stars of tennis. Much later, from 1996 to 2006, when British player, Tim Henman, was engaged in a tight Wimbledon singles match, the crowds would melt away from the other courts and gather opposite the big screen on the large grass mound which came to be known as 'Henman Hill.' Hillyard describes a similar phenomenon with the Renshaws, more than a hundred years earlier:

Who that witnessed the lawn tennis of the (eighteen) eighties doesn't remember the Renshaw rush? When whatever match was in progress, and however exciting it might be, the moment the famous twins appeared on the scene, the whole gallery arose as one man, and there was a perfect stampede of spectators and chairs to whatever court they were going to play on.

The following year, Hillyard, with Lewis again, lost to the Renshaws in Dublin. He also lost the first round of the singles and of the mixed. Having exited the singles he was entitled to take part in the Fitzwilliam Purse, where he again reached the final, losing this time to D. G. Chaytor.

A major achievement this year was winning the British covered court doubles title with Scrivener, which he would successfully defend in 1891.

He went out in the second round at Wimbledon, losing again to Barlow. In the doubles he paired with Lewis. They had a comfortable straight sets win against Mahoney and Barlow, but lost the all-comers final to Joshua Pim and Frank Stoker by a disappointing 0-6, 5-7, 4-6.

At Chiswick Park he didn't enter the open singles but lost in the handicap semi to A. W. Gore, a future Wimbledon champion – at this time even the top players regularly played in handicap events. In doubles, he partnered Lewis and reached the final before going down to the Baddeley twins. The pair also played together at Queen's Club and reached the semis.

Hillyard travelled with Lord Hawke's cricket team to America in 1891. The tour began in September and that summer he played more cricket and less competitive tennis. The same was to be true in 1894 when he toured America again. He decided not to enter Wimbledon, but at the back end of the year, just before his trip, he had one of his best singles wins to date, beating D. G. Chaytor at Eastbourne before falling to Barlow in a four set semi. In the doubles he partnered Ernest Renshaw and went out early. As usual at Eastbourne, Hillyard paired up with his wife in the mixed, and the two made it through to the final before losing to Barlow and Miss Langrishe.

The most prolific tournament of the Hillyards was Eastbourne – a seaside event they rarely missed. This and the next 2 photos are from the family album. All are in 1904. To the left is the semi of the mixed, George Hillyard up this end, watching partner, Miss Douglas (later Mrs Lambert Chambers) about to hit a smash. The opponents are Sidney Smith and Miss Thomson.

Here is the mixed final at Eastbourne – Hillyard and Douglas (later Mrs Lambert Chambers) both facing the camera, were the winners.
Surely the spectators sitting up to the court on the right-hand side would have been in the way for anyone chasing a wide ball.

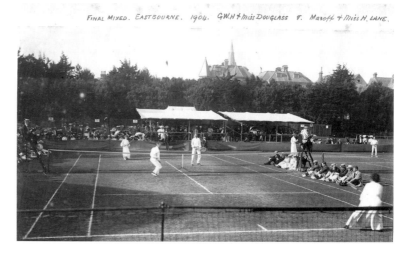

Here is the men's final at Eastbourne in 1904 – a win for Hillyard and Smith. At this end are the famously identical Allen twins, wearing identical attire, haircuts and large tummies.
Again there are spectators sitting dangerously close to the court – even more this time!

He returned to Wimbledon in 1892 but lost in his first match against friend and doubles partner Ernest Lewis. That year he had a good win at the Irish Championships, beating Mahoney, before losing to Frank Stoker in the quarters. He then lost to Mahoney in the semis at Leicester, and to Pim in the semis of the handicap. He partnered C. S. Viccars in the doubles, only to lose in the semis. At Hyde Park he lost in the second round to H. A. Chapman. Also in this year, as reported in the New York Times, the American player Oliver Campbell toured Britain for the first time. His opening tournament was The Northern, where he beat Hillyard. Partnering Ernest Renshaw, Hillyard returned the compliment in the doubles. The pair progressed to the final of the all-comers where they lost to Stoker and Pim. Later, at Wimbledon, Hillyard paired up with the American, but lost early on. To complete his efforts in the Northern, he partnered Blanche in the mixed and reached the semis, losing to Lottie Dod and her brother, Tony.

Hillyard lost the second round at Wimbledon 1893, against Irishman Manville Goodbody in a five-setter, 6-4, 3-6, 8-6, 6-8, 2-6. In doubles he partnered Barlow but lost the first match. He reached the final of the Leicester tournament, but retired after losing the first set 6-1 to Pim. On the way to the final he had beaten Mahoney.

He reached the final of the all-comers singles at Eastbourne where he lost to Wilfred Baddeley 6-3, 6-3, 6-1. Earlier, in the third round, he had beaten Herbert Baddeley in straight sets. Partnering C. G. Ball-Greene, he went out to the Baddeleys in the third round.

At this time Hillyard began playing regular representative cricket for Leicestershire and consequently played less competitive tennis until 1896, the year of his move into Thorpe Satchville. Nevertheless, in 1894 he still played at Dublin where he and Blanche won the mixed title against C. H. Martin and Miss C. Cooper (later Mrs Stery). At Wimbledon he only entered the doubles, with old friend, Clem Cazalet. In the quarters they beat Gore and Palmer, to whom Hillyard had lost in the previous year with a different partner, but then went out to the Baddeleys in straight sets.

At the Northern Championships, Hillyard lost to Chapman in the semi of the all-comers singles having beaten Mahoney in four sets in the round before. In the doubles he partnered Cazalet and reached the final, falling again to the Baddeleys.

From 1895 he took a two-season break from Wimbledon, but did enter Eastbourne. This year he won the all-comers title, defeating Herbert Baddeley 1-6, 6-4, 6-3, 6-2, having beaten Laurie Doherty in the first round 6-3, 6-2, and Ball-Greene in the quarters. In the challenge final he lost once more to W. Baddeley. Having shared the first two sets 6-3, 7-9, he retired after losing a tough third set 7-5.

In the men's doubles he partnered Chaytor to the final against the Baddeley twins. The match could not be completed and the prize was shared. Hillyard capped off a successful week by the sea with a win in the mixed doubles partnering Blanche.

1896, the date of his move into Thorpe Satchville, was a busier tennis year for George Hillyard although it started badly in Dublin. Then, at the Northern Championships, he won the all-comers doubles with Cazalet, beating the Allen twins in the final only to lose to the Baddeleys in the championship round.

Returning once more to Eastbourne, he reached the doubles final with Smith where they shared the title with the Baddeleys, and made the semis of the singles but gave H. Baddeley a walkover.

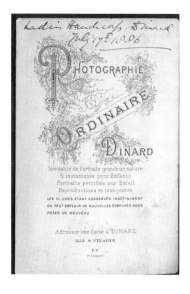

A faded postcard of Dinard, from Hillyard's album. On the back is written "Ladies Handicap Final July 17th 1896"

He had a very good tournament at Monte Carlo, winning the singles, doubles, singles handicap, and the mixed (with Blanche). Writing a year later, on May 12 1897, Charles Voigt from the American LTA said of the French Riviera: *Here, year after year, the famous twin brothers Renshaw, to whom the game and its popularity owe so much, Hillyard and Mrs Hillyard, and a host of others, may be found.* He then mentions that this year Hillyard had to return to England before the Monte Carlo tournament started: *The absence of G.W. and Mrs Hillyard who last year won most of the prizes, was deeply regretted.*

He returned to Wimbledon in 1897, winning two rounds before going out to Sidney Smith in the quarters. In the doubles he partnered Mahoney and they reached the semis where they lost to the Dohertys. This year he also played in Nice, and lost again to Smith in the quarters of the Irish Championships. He didn't enter the mixed and went out in the first round of the men's with Ball-Greene.

More notably, the first International Championship of Germany was held this year, and Hillyard took the title, battling against his erstwhile doubles partner, G. C. Ball-Greene in a five-set singles final, before managing to close out the last two sets 6-0, 6-0.

At the Northern, Hillyard lost in the singles semi to Reggie Doherty, and the doubles semi, partnering Mahoney, to the Riseleys. At Eastbourne he lost to Laurie Doherty in a terrific semi-final, 7-9, 6-2, 6-3, 4-6, 6-2. In the doubles with Chaytor they made the final and lost to the Dohertys. With Blanche in the mixed he went out in the semis.

At Wimbledon 1898, he was defeated by Laurie Doherty in the second round. The year before, just eight years after Willie Renshaw's final victory at Wimbledon, Laurie's brother, R. F. (Reggie) Doherty, had added his name to the Championship Roll. The two Dohertys dominated the 1890s and beyond just as the Renshaws dominated the 1880s.

Laurie and Reggie Doherty, in style and athleticism, were a step on from the Renshaws. Naturally each generation makes progress, and the highest-class tennis of 110 years ago would be very different from that of today. But in their time, the Dohertys were the most complete players, and would be recognisable as such even now. As a possible point of reference, imagine a Group One county match of 30 years ago – played on grass, slice serves to a length, one-handed backhands, solid returns and deep first volleys. This was the classic style of the Dohertys, and it brought huge success - between them they won the Wimbledon singles title nine times, and the doubles title eight times as a pair,

The period following the Renshaws had seen a decline in the number of spectators at Wimbledon, but the advent of the Dohertys reversed this decline, and then brought about a new surge in popularity which has continued to the present day.

The Dohertys suffered from health problems throughout their lives, and were encouraged by their father to take up tennis when young to help with respiratory illness. Reggie Doherty, in particular, was often sick, and confided to Hillyard 'I don't know what it is, George, to feel really well.'

The brothers were famous for their sportsmanship on court. Reggie Doherty was with Hillyard when he captained a tour of South Africa in 1908/09. Although unwell through much of an arduous schedule, Reggie barely lost a match and was feted wherever he went. His style was quite relaxed compared with his compatriots, and it was said he had to run less because of his superb anticipation (although this was probably more to do with his superior standard of hitting and placement, making it difficult for opponents to put him under pressure). As Myers said: *Throughout the whole of George Hillyard's long South African tour R. F. used the same pair of rubber shoes, while every other member of the team wore out several pairs.*

Absolutely one of my favourite photos from Thorpe Satchville A private 'friendly' doubles featuring Hillyard and the Dohertys pauses whilst the players argue Hillyard with hands clasped behind his back listens to Laurie Doherty explaining what happened. Brother Reggie keeps well out of it!

Hillyard recalled 'I was honoured with their closest friendship for many years.' When speaking of the brothers, he is not just a fan but also a long-standing comrade. Like the Renshaws, the Dohertys had quite different styles of play. Reggie was very tall and, according to Hillyard, Laurie was quite short. In fact Laurie was reputedly five foot ten inches but to the taller Hillyard this may have seemed small. The brothers enjoyed competing against each other in private but less so in match play. As a doubles pair they lost only four times in ten years of competition between 1897 and 1906 (when they mostly gave up serious tennis). One of these losses was against Hillyard, partnering Ball-Greene in Homburg. Hillyard also tells of a match in 1902, partnering Cazalet in the final at Queen's Club, where he contrived to lose despite having held nine match points including a return from Laurie Doherty that was going out when it hit the net post and dribbled back over the net for a winner. This said, and as noted earlier, Hillyard was the type of player susceptible to squandering winning leads.

A posed photo of the great Laurie Doherty from Hillyard's album. I'm unsure of the venue, but matches are in progress behind.

Reggie Doherty went on to win the Olympic Doubles gold medal with Hillyard in 1908, but two years later he died at the age of 38. George Hillyard was a principal mourner at the funeral. Brother Laurie, who was three years younger than his brother, had mostly given up tennis in 1906 to play golf. He continued to spend many hours on Hillyard's private golf course in the grounds at Thorpe Satchville. Laurie also died tragically young, aged only 43. The memory of the two brothers is today celebrated in the Doherty Gates, at the south-west entrance to the All England Club, presented in 1930 by their elder brother the Rev. William Doherty.

Back to 1898, and Hillyard reached the challenge round of the German Championships, but lost early in the singles at Monte Carlo, the Northern and the South of England championships. In the Wimbledon doubles he partnered Sidney Smith and they reached the all-comers final before losing disappointingly in four sets to Clarence Hobart and Harold Nisbet. At Eastbourne he and Nisbet won the doubles in a memorable five-set final against Smith and Greville, 8-6, 4-6, 4-6, 6-2, 6-2. This might have gone some small way to make up for losing to Blanche in the third round of the mixed! At the Northern Championships he also did well in the doubles, partnering Smith to a place in the final where they went out to the Dohertys. In addition, he and Blanche reached the final of the mixed.

Michael Charles, the current owner of 'Thorpe Satchville', and the author, standing outside the front door where the Doherty brothers stood more than a hundred years before.

Hillyard again partnered Smith at Wimbledon in 1899, but lost in the quarters. He continued his unimpressive singles record at the Championships, giving a walkover to Greville in the second round, but was subsequently allowed to enter the All England Plate. This was an event for first-round losers, initiated in 1896 to encourage a higher level of singles entry. In 1895 they had received only 18 entries in the men's singles and recorded Wimbledon's one and only financial loss – to the tune of £33. The Plate event was to survive for another 85 years before being discontinued. In 1899 Hillyard reached the final, but then gave a walkover after an argument with officialdom over scheduling.

On December 6th, 1899, the LTA published a judgement, titled 'The report of the Committee appointed to investigate the complaint of Mr G. W. Hillyard against the referee and committee of the All England Championship Meeting, 1899.'

Hillyards' complaint was in 3 parts:

After losing a long match in the doubles semi, he was asked on the same afternoon to play his singles final in the Plate. When he refused he was scratched, despite offering to play the next day (the concluding day of the tournament), or any other day that week at his opponent's convenience.

In calling him to play his doubles at 3pm the Committee departed from the previous order of play.

If the Committee intended him to play both matches on the Monday, then the Plate singles final should have been played before the doubles.

Evidence was given by Archie Palmer on behalf of the Club, and by George Hillyard.

The judgement is too long to print here. It was agreed that on the Saturday Hillyard had been told the Plate final would be held at 3pm on Monday with the doubles to follow. By Monday the Committee had changed their minds. The doubles event was running behind and they decided to play the semi at 3pm, with the Plate afterwards.

No-one told Hillyard of the change. Having lost a long and hard-fought doubles match, he came off court exhausted and was upset to be told he should then play his singles.

Of course, had he won his doubles it is possible that the all-comers final would have taken place straight after, as Hillyard believed was the original intention. In the event, however, the Committee put on the doubles with Hillyard's victors, and then insisted that his Plate opponent was on the ground and waiting. In response to Hillyard's offer to play the next day, he was told his opponent had already said that he would be unavailable.

The LTA backed the Wimbledon Committee. Their most telling argument was that the onus had been on Hillyard to find out when his Plate final would be taking place. If he had asked, he would have been told. They therefore ruled against him and published the result of their deliberations in *Lawn Tennis Magazine*. In practice they may have had split sympathies. In the modern era, the singles would have been put off to the next day, rather than be scheduled directly after a doubles. And if his opponent was unavailable on any day within the dates of the tournament, then he would have been the one scratched – not Hillyard.

At Eastbourne he lost in the singles semi to Mahoney, but continued his impressive record on the south coast with a win in the doubles with Cazalet and the mixed with Blanche.

Hillyard had always been successful at doubles but in 1900 he continued his improvement at singles. He began by winning the German International Championships. With Cazalet he lost in the doubles final, and with Blanche in the mixed final. He then travelled to Homburg where he lost the final to Laurie Doherty, having previously achieved a famous win against brother Reggie. He lost to Laurie at Cannes, and again in the final at Monte Carlo. He reached the doubles final with Eaves only to lose once more to the Dohertys.

Back home he won the Northumberland championships, and made the final of the doubles with Cazalet, again losing to the Dohertys. He had another run through to the final at Eastbourne, and lost to Laurie Doherty. He and Cazalet had no more luck in the doubles final against the Dohertys and he lost in the semi of the mixed with Blanche. He didn't enter the Wimbledon singles, but partnered Cazalet in the doubles where they lost to Nisbet and Roper Barrett in the semis.

1901 was to be another busy and successful year. In the Wimbledon doubles with Wilberforce Eaves he lost his first match to Dwight Davis and Holcombe Ward. This was an interesting encounter – Ward and Davis were American players visiting Britain for the first time. They arrived in England with a new weapon – the American twist serve – basically a fast, kicking topspin which would have moved away from the returner, in the opposite direction to the slice that the British were used to.

Dwight Davis, partner of Holcombe Ward, but most famous as the man who invented the Davis Cup competition and donated the trophy, buying it with his own money for $1,000 Here he is playing tennis at Thorpe Satchville as a guest of the Hillyards, in the year he and his partner introduced the American twist serve to England

Hillyard takes up the story: *Towards the end of May, Dwight Davis and Holcombe Ward, Doubles champions of America, had arrived in England for the purpose of an attack on Wimbledon. The first thing I knew of their arrival was a letter from 'The Doctor'* (W. Eaves – Hillyard's upcoming partner at Wimbledon that year), *who himself had just come over from America, telling me he had laid Davis a level 'tenner' that we could beat them in a private match, and would I ask them all down to Thorpe for a weekend with that object in view. Would I not, indeed!*

An invitation was quickly despatched, and in due course our guests arrived. We had heard vague rumours of their wonderful service, the likes of which had never been seen, and that it was quite untakeable by ordinary mortals, etc, etc. The following day was devoted to some quiet practice, in order that our guests might become accustomed to the court and conditions. Of course we were all agog to see the much-talked-of serve, but divil a glimpse did we get to see of it! That was a little surprise packet they were keeping strictly up their sleeves, and only to be produced at the Championship Meeting! This was a disappointment. However there are compensations, even in a disappointing world; and the following day, 8th June, the Doctor and I defeated them, minus their service, three sets to love, 6-2, 6-4, 6-1, and repeated the performance on the 9th (in the best of three sets) 6-2, 6-1. The next time we met was at the Championship Meeting. There with the aid of the American service, which in that match was unmasked for the first time, they had their revenge, defeating us after a terrific fight, 3-6, 6-3, 11-9, 9-7. In almost every department of the game we were their masters, with the exception of the service, but that just tipped the balance in their favour. It certainly was an exceedingly awkward serve to deal with at the first time of asking.

W. Eaves ('The Doctor') who partnered Hillyard at Wimbledon (and Thorpe Satchville) against the American invaders, Ward and Davis. Here he is at Thorpe, schoolroom in the background.

Blanche Hillyard with another American invader at Thorpe – the first overseas player to win Wimbledon, May Sutton

I particularly like Hillyard's line: *'In almost every department of the game we were their masters.'* I wonder if the Americans agreed! In the event they then reached the challenge round without dropping another set, but were defeated by three sets to one by the Dohertys in what Hillyard described as 'a stern struggle.'

The notion that the Americans had a secret weapon that they refused to unveil in practice but instead kept back until the first real test at the Championships … how wonderful!

In the Wimbledon singles of 1901 Hillyard finally did himself some justice, beating Laurie Doherty in the third round before losing to Arthur Gore in the quarters after a thrilling five-setter, 1-6, 6-2, 6-4, 6-8, 2-6. In fact, this was to be the closest he ever came to being crowned Wimbledon singles champion. Reggie Doherty was the previous year's champion, awaiting the all-comers winner, but he was ill and only put up token resistance in the Challenge final.

Wallis Myers relates: *Indeed, the match between Gore and George Hillyard in a previous round (a match which Hillyard had good cause to remember for he lost it by a net-cord) was regarded, even at the time, as the gate to the throne.* In other words both Hillyard and Gore knew beforehand that the winner of their match would be the favourite to end up champion. Myers says: *Hillyard opposed Gore under a fierce sun, and at one time was leading by two sets to one, five games to four and forty-love. At this critical juncture Gore drove a ball that hit the net, hesitated one breathless second as to which side it should fall, then jumped down over Hillyard's outstretched racket. Had the ball fallen on the other side or had it come over in the ordinary way, another name would probably have been added to the Championship roll.*

But of course, even after Gore had his slice of good fortune, the score was still 5-4 and 40-15 to Hillyard, with two match points remaining. Had he kept his cool and believed he was destined to win (rather than taking the net-cord as proof he was destined to lose!), he would still have been favourite. Instead he lost his temper, and with it the championships.

As Myers also related on another occasion: *it was at Brighton where Hillyard was so upset at the remarkably defective umpiring which caused him the loss of an important match that to calm his ruffled feelings he strode down to the beach and sat down under the brow of a breakwater. Hours passed and the other events in which the present All England secretary was competing were entirely ignored. At length Hillyard rose in a more philosophical frame of mind and returned slowly to the ground. He was met by the secretary who offered him the sympathy he deserved.*

Despite appearances, this last sentence was not intended to be ironic – Hillyard *was* offered sympathy for the perceived poor umpiring. Whether someone nowadays who disappeared off the ground with matches still to play would be offered any kind of sympathy, deserved or otherwise, by the tournament secretary is a moot point!

George Hillyard in action.
Not a bad throwing action on the serve, and a big forehand about to be hit!

Arthur Gore went on to win the Championship in 1901 after his victory over Hillyard, and was to win again in 1908 and 1909. He was no relation to Spencer Gore, the first winner of the title in 1877. Spencer Gore was an able sportsman who picked up a racquet and found himself an unlikely champion of a newly invented game. Arthur Gore was a hard-working businessman, unable to focus his whole life on tennis in the way that some of his contemporaries were able to – but he was a tennis player through and through, eventually making a record thirty appearances at Wimbledon. He was also the oldest player, at 41, ever to hold the title, and the last British player to do so until Fred Perry embarked upon his hat-trick in 1934.

Gore had an immense forehand, a true weapon. As Hillyard said: *Gore's backhand was comparatively weak, but it was a very difficult matter to force him to take a ball on that wing, as he was very quick and light on his feet, and had wonderfully good anticipation.* Once again we find specific styles of player turning up at the dawn of tennis, much the same as in the modern game. Hillyard's description of Gore could just as easily be used for Steffi Graf, or Jim Courier. There is a photograph of Gore playing Wilding on centre court, and Gore is standing well outside the tramline on the left-hand side of the court, hitting an inside out forehand. I remember watching Courier at Wembley in London near the start of his career, and he constantly did the same, almost refusing to hit a backhand unless absolutely forced to do so. Of course, his versatility improved as he made his way up the rankings to world number one, and I am certain that Courier's playing standard would have been much higher than Gore's, but the *tactical* style of play is the same.

The rather basic nature of a journey to Portugal is described with real humour in Hillyard's book. Once there he won the Portuguese Championships, beating Clem Cazalet in the semis, and Harold Mahoney in the final. He also won the doubles with Cazalet.

At Cannes he again lost to Laurie Doherty, having reached the final after Reggie gave him a walkover in the round before. This is likely to have been a tactical concession due to the brothers not liking to meet in match play.

In the same year Hillyard gave walkovers at Nice and at Queens before reaching the semis of the Northern championships where he lost to Eaves. At Buxton he partnered Laurie Doherty to the doubles title, and then lost to him in the final of the singles. Moving on to his favourite Eastbourne event, he and Cazalet won the doubles, but he went out in the last eight of the singles.

Hillyard and Blanche were about to embark for Germany to defend his title in the German Championships when they heard of the death of Empress Friedrich. Believing wrongly that the Championships would be cancelled, they returned home and, in consequence, Hillyard conceded a walkover to Max Decugis in the Challenge Round.

1902 was another strong competitive year for Hillyard, even though he was now 38. At Wimbledon he lost in the third round to Major J. G. Ritchie, having retired after two sets with honours even.

Major Ritchie wasn't a Major in the military sense – Major was his first name. In writings from the time, he is mostly referred to as simply 'Ritchie.' Ritchie was a steady, controlled British player of the first rank who won the Wimbledon doubles twice, partnering Tony Wilding. He also won a Gold medal for singles at the 1908 Olympics. He was considered a master of the baseline game and had particular success in German tournaments. He named his son Richard and, clearly inspired by having such a great name, Richard Ritchie went on to be Secretary of Queens Club for 30 years.

Hillyard partnered Clem Cazalet in the Wimbledon doubles again. They reached the all-comers final where they narrowly lost in five sets to Riseley and Smith who then scored a famous five-set victory over the Dohertys in the Challenge round, winning 11-9 in the final set.

At Monte Carlo, Hillyard reached the final only to lose to Reggie Doherty. He went out to Cazalet at Leicester, but then partnered him to the doubles final before losing to the Dohertys again. He reached the final of the Homburg Coronation Cup then lost to Ritchie. Again he decided to concede, this time after winning the first set but losing the next two of a five-setter. He promptly lost once more to Ritchie at a second tournament in Homburg, this time in the semis. The match was only a three-setter and he managed to go the distance for a 4-6, 7-5, 3-6 scoreline.

The European Championships followed and Hillyard reached the semis again, losing a tight match to old friend Harold Mahoney. In the doubles he partnered Cazalet and lost in the final to the Dohertys having won the first two sets, 6-3, 7-5, 8-10, 3-6, 7-9.

Hillyard won the Buxton title by beating Ball-Greene in a five set final. He managed a clean sweep, partnering the same man to win the men's doubles and Miss Robb to win the mixed. At Eastbourne he was less successful, losing to Ritchie in the quarters and failing to make any doubles finals.

Arthur Myers, writing in his excellent book 'Lawn Tennis at Home and Abroad' in 1903, described Hillyard as follows:

Both cricket and tennis have claimed George Hillyard as their votary, and in both has he excelled. Tall and distinguished, finely built, and strong as a lion, it would indeed be a surprise if outdoor sports did not claim Hillyard as an expert. He was showing me his photographic album one day, and I received reliable evidence that his versatility extended to golf, at which game he has won several prizes, among other places at Cannes. He began to play lawn tennis after he left the Navy, and during the last fifteen years has rarely failed to put in an appearance at all the principal meetings in England, while his pilgrimages abroad have been both many and fruitful, and on two occasions he has been returned Champion of Germany. It should not be forgotten that Hillyard was within an ace of beating Gore at Wimbledon in 1901, the ball hitting the top of the net and rolling over on the wrong side. Had it fallen on the right Hillyard might have been Champion of England! … .. His low cross fore-hand drive, which so often scores outright, his enormous reach, and high muscular service — above all, his stamina, are professional equipments that any man might envy. In private life G. W. Hillyard is a modest and amiable gentleman with a host of friends. On his private tennis courts at Thorpe Satchville, the delightful home of Mr. and Mrs. Hillyard near Melton Mowbray, most of the leading players of to-day have appeared and contested matches, the records of which would if kept, I doubt not, make very interesting reading.

Mexico City 1903
Mrs Butlin
Miss Butlin
C.H.L.C
GWH

Here's an oddity. Hillyard played fewer tournaments in 1903 but he did, it seems, find time to travel to Mexico City with good tennis friend Claude Cazalet. Here the two men stand behind, and flanking, the rather attractive Miss Butlin, whoever Miss Butlin may be.

No. 341   es - propiedad, depositada 15 abril 1902   A. Briquet, fot.
Orizaba, Hotel de France el Patio.   ESTADO DE VERA-CRUZ   Orizaba, Court of Hotel France.

Also found in the Hillyard album – a post card of the Hotel France in Mexico City. A trip not mentioned in any other writing I could find, it is to be hoped that Hillyard had a good time in Mexico!

Hillyard played less tennis in 1903. He lost in the first round of the Longwood tournament, and then scratched from the South of France and Monte Carlo tournaments. At the Queens Spring Covered Court championships he won the all-comers, beating Mahoney in the final, before a loss to Laurie Doherty in the challenge round.

He didn't enter Wimbledon that year, but he did in 1904, although just doubles, partnered by Cazalet again and losing in five sets in the quarters against a Belgian pair. At the Northumberland championships he went out to Laurie Doherty, and then to Smith in the quarters at Eastbourne.

He partnered Laurie Doherty to the Indoor Championships at Queens, and was to repeat that success the following year. At Edgbaston he lost early to Ritchie and partnered Eaves to the doubles semi, losing to Smith and Riseley. He had a good win against Tony Wilding in the first round at Buxton before losing in the semis. With Eaves he won the doubles and partnered Blanche to the semis of the mixed. At Eastbourne he lost in the quarters to Smith but together they took the doubles title, beating the Allen twins in the final. He also paired with Miss Dorothea Douglas (later Mrs Lambert Chambers) for the mixed title.

At Wimbledon 1905, Hillyard and Cazalet lost to Brookes in the doubles over five sets, but in the singles he beat his doubles partner before succumbing to another tennis 'great', Norman Brookes, in straight sets, 6-3, 6-1, 6-3.

In 1907 Norman Brookes became the first player from outside the United Kingdom to win the Wimbledon singles title. He was to regain it in 1914, beating Tony Wilding in the Challenge Round. Brookes was the first of the long line of great Australian players. He was a wily left-hander who became a good friend of Hillyard, and stayed regularly at Thorpe Satchville. His influence over Australian tennis was unparalleled, and he became the first President of the Australian Lawn Tennis Association, a position he held for 28 years.

The above photos are not identified in Hillyard's album but they have the feel of a hot country with the children behind wearing wide hats. The courts look like clay and there is no fencing behind.

In 1904 the Hillyards joined Leicester Lawn Tennis Club which later became known as Leicestershire Lawn Tennis Club. This began a long association between them and the club, centring on the annual Leicester tournament. The applications for all new members had to be considered and approved (or black-balled!), at committee meetings

Here is the minute of the Leicester LTC committee meeting in April 1904 when they were officially approved as members. As befits a Wimbledon champion and her husband, their names top the list

Norman Brookes, the first great Australian Wimbledon champion, at Leicester, possibly in 1907.
He is left-handed, but look at the technique on the volley!

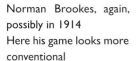

Norman Brookes, again, possibly in 1914
Here his game looks more conventional

Back to 1905 and Hillyard reached the final of the Bad Homburg Tournament in Germany, eventually going down 7-5 in the 5th set to Tony Wilding. At Dinard, in France, Hillyard reached the final of the singles, only to lose to Norman Brookes again. Back in England, he performed superbly at his local tournament, winning the singles at Leicester with a victory over Eaves. Partnering Clem, he then lost to Eaves and Reggie Doherty, but won the mixed with Miss Pinckney.

Harold Mahoney, Hillyard's great friend, sadly died on 27th June 1905 near his home in Kerry, Ireland. He was knocked off his bicycle and died of his injuries.

This picture of Mahoney is from the Hillyard's own album. In the top left hand corner is the date "1905", presumably in Hillyard's hand, to mark the year of his friend's death.

He partnered A. W. Dunlop to the Buxton doubles title, and lost in the mixed final with Miss Douglas. He lost in a 3-set semi at Edgbaston to Brookes having managed to win a set. He then partnered Brookes to the doubles, beating Ritchie and Smith. The mixed with Miss Douglass was shared with the final unfinished.

The following year Hillyard conceded walkovers at Wimbledon and the British Hard Courts to Arthur Gore. However, he did then win the Singles Plate competition at Wimbledon – on the two occasions he gave walkovers in the first round at Wimbledon he went on to reach the final of the Plate event. Quite a neat way of gaining an entry!

He later reached the semis of the European Championships at Leicester and of the Midlands Championships. He came away from the Northumberland event with both singles and mixed doubles titles, beating Eaves for the former and partnering the American May Sutton in the latter. At Edgbaston he lost to Eaves in the semi, and then partnered him to win the doubles.

Back to Germany and Hillyard reached the semis at Homburg, going out to Tony Wilding, and the semis again at Baden-Baden, before returning to England to reach the semis at Eastbourne, losing to Tony Wilding. Even at 42 years of age, Hillyard was still managing to compete at the very highest level. It is noticeable in this roll call of players how the names that he plays against change. He is the one who competes across generations.

Tony Wilding was a New Zealander who won the Australian Championships in 1906 and 1909, as well as the Wimbledon Doubles in 1907 and 1908, but really shot to world fame on winning the Wimbledon singles championship four years running, from 1910 through to 1913. He was a young, dashing barrister (although he never actually practised as one, preferring to play tennis and enjoy himself), a first class cricketer, a golfer, and a man who loved to ride his motorbike on epic journeys around Europe. He was a media celebrity – at the time of his death in 1915 in France during the Great War he was engaged to Hollywood actress, Maxine Elliott – and a close friend of the Hillyards. He spent many days at their home in Thorpe Satchville, playing tennis, golf, and any other sport on offer.

Tony Wilding at Thorpe Satchville, next to another great champion Lambert Chambers. Probably taken around 1905, she was already twice Wimbledon champion although still unmarried when the photo was taken. Wilding looks tense!

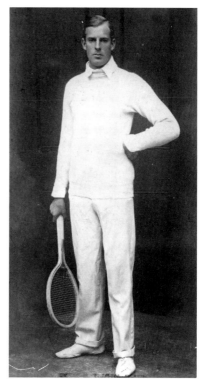

Wilding again, more relaxed. About to embark on 4 straight wins of the Wimbledon singles title

1907 was a milestone. George Hillyard became Secretary of The All England Club at Wimbledon. He never entered the Championship singles again, perhaps feeling that he didn't have the time to combine it with his official duties. Maybe he considered winning the Plate in the previous year a reasonable finale. His appointment didn't seem to restrict him otherwise. He partnered Norman Brookes in the Covered Court Championships at Queens, losing in the final to Simond and Reggie Doherty. At Leicester he partnered Reggie but lost to Brookes and Eaves in the final. Throughout the tournament it rained so much that this was the only event completed.

He won the singles at Eastbourne, beating Crawley in the final. He won the doubles with Brookes, and then partnered the newly married Mrs Lambert Chambers to a defeat in the mixed final against Blanche and Norman Brookes.

At Newcastle he lost to Eaves in the semi, and then the pair of them lost the doubles final to Brookes and G. Sharp. This time he won the mixed with Mrs Lambert Chambers, beating Blanche and Brookes in the final 7-5, 2-6, 6-3.

Photo.   *Miss Kendall, Leicester.*

G. C. Ball-Greene and W. V. Eaves playing in the Doubles at Leicester on Court I. They were beaten in the final by R. F. Doherty and G. W. Hillyard.

A picture and description from "Lawn Tennis and Badminton" in 1908. In the bottom right hand corner it says in tiny print 'Miss Kendall *(sic)*, Leicester'. Yes indeed – the great aunt of the same Mr Kendal who brought the photos to Michael at Thorpe Satchville and told him of the house's history.

A county final at Leicestershire Club in 2007 – large crowds sitting on the roof of the 'new' pavilion, built in 1930, having replaced the one in the photo from 1908.

By 1908 Hillyard was 44, but still reached two major singles finals, at Yorkshire and Eastbourne. He lost one to Laurie Doherty and the other to Tony Wilding – two of the greatest players of the age. He also had good wins at Leicester, beating Crawley in the singles final, and partnering Reggie Doherty to the doubles title. Reggie and he were also successful at Nottingham.

Father and son, playing doubles together at Felixstowe in 1908

Hillyard played Felixstowe this year, winning the singles and the mixed with Lambert Chambers. He also paired up for the first time in an open tournament with his son, Jack - the father and son combination losing in the second round. In a report on the meeting it was noted: 'J. Hillyard showed promising form and won the second class handicap.'

In Newcastle he won the doubles with Eaves and the mixed with Lambert Chambers having lost the singles in the final.

He returned to the Wimbledon doubles event, despite being Club Secretary - presumably the lure was just too much to resist. He partnered Cazalet and they did well, getting through to the semis where they met the eventual champions, Tony Wilding and Ritchie. Once more it was a five-set battle, going down

3-6, 6-4, 6-4, 5-7, 5-7. They were within a point of victory and there is every chance that had they won this match they would have gone on to win the trophy as there was no challenge final that year. With so many near misses to look back upon, Hillyard might by now have considered himself fated never to be a champion at Wimbledon.

This said, 1908 was also the year that George Hillyard partnered Reggie Doherty to the Olympics Doubles title. Not a bad effort for a man of 44!

In the winter of 1908/09 Hillyard was selected as captain of the Great Britain team that toured South Africa. On his return, he again won the Leicester doubles title with Cazalet. With Miss Morton, Hillyard lost in the final of the mixed to Reggie Doherty and Mrs Winch. The Dohertys put in a rare appearance at Nottingham in the invitation doubles – Hillyard lost to them in the semis.

Hillyard and Cazalet once more paired up at Wimbledon but lost early in the second round. In total they were partners seven times at Wimbledon and this was their last outing.

The following year Hillyard reached the final at Felixstowe where he lost to Roper Barrett. At Nottingham he went out in the third round but reached the final of the mixed with Blanche, the title being shared. They also won the Married Couples championship.

He reached the invitation doubles final at Nottingham In 1911, partnering the French player A. Gobert against Dixon and Doust. Burrow said: *It resolved itself into a question of whether Hillyard could nurse Gobert through or not; in the end he just failed, but only after a most brilliant exhibition on his own part. Gobert was at that time just 21 - a fine but not seasoned player. He was not playing well and the worse he played the sadder he became. 'Ah, no! Hillyard. I cannot play. Let's scratch. You see, I cannot play. I feel so bad 'ere!' he kept exclaiming, with appropriate gestures. But Hillyard encouraged him so nobly that it was only 6-4 in the fifth set that Doust and Dixon scraped home.*

Later, Hillyard partnered Beamish to the doubles final at Leicester where they lost to Eaves and Heath.

1912 brought a very personal triumph – the Hillyards won the All-England Married Couples Championship at Nottingham for the third year running, and therefore the Cup outright, in the year of their silver wedding anniversary.

Come 1913 Hillyard was back at Eastbourne partnering Parke to the doubles final where they lost in four sets to Prebble and Doust. He also made his last appearance at Wimbledon. It was the offer of partnering Tony Wilding that brought him out of retirement. What an occasion it must have been – Hillyard was 49 years old and Tony Wilding just 29 and at the peak of his powers, having been Wimbledon singles champion since 1910. The younger man was the matinee idol of tennis, with women queuing up to get his autograph on every appearance. Although he and Hillyard lost in the quarters to a regulation pairing of Beamish and Parke, Wilding had nothing at all to prove, and the five-set match would have made good entertainment.

Local legend 'Bertie' Buckler, who lost to Hillyard in the open mixed doubles at Leicester in 1919 Hillyard was 55 years old and won the event.

This was also the year that Wilding beat Maurice McLoughlin, 'the Californian Comet', in what was described at the time as the greatest final ever seen. For Hillyard the doubles loss must have been bitter-sweet. A pleasure to partner Wilding, yet a frustration to lose yet another Wimbledon match, his final one, and once again in five sets.

At Leicester, Hillyard entered the singles and lost to Gore in the final, a veteran's match in an open event. Partnering Gore they also lost the final. He and Parke reached the final at Eastbourne where they lost to Prebble and Doust.

Eastbourne was cancelled in 1914 with the outbreak of war. Nottingham took place and Hillyard reached the doubles final with Dixon, losing to Gore and Crisp, while with Blanche he again won the Married Couples event.

After the war, on July 10th 1919, the Leicester tournament was revived and Hillyard entered. Despite being 55 years old, he won the mixed doubles with Mrs Lamplough – what a great effort! Of purely parochial interest, they beat Mr and Mrs H. A. Buckler in the first round. Mr Buckler was a legendary longstanding member of the Leicester club, who lived across the road and originally paid for the construction of the club's all-weather Court 13, still referred to as 'The Buckler court'.

In the same tournament Hillyard partnered his son, Jack, in the doubles and reached the semi-final. One can imagine the crowds gathering around to watch the famous Wimbledon Club Secretary, veteran of so many high-quality matches at Leicester and far beyond, partnering his son. This was probably the perfect moment for Hillyard to stop and reflect on his career in competitive tennis – full of incident, full of success (and also some failure); a career of contest, of travel, and of friendship.

A wonderful tennis life.

7

EARLY WIMBLEDON AND HILLYARD'S ROLE
IN THE FOUNDING OF THE LTA

As mentioned earlier, Henry Jones, Julian Marshall and C. G. Heathcote were the three men who crafted the first set of generally accepted rules of lawn tennis in 1877. Each remained an influential character in those early years when public awareness of tennis in Britain was largely shaped by people and events surrounding Wimbledon. The fortunes of the sport and of the All England Club were inextricably linked. Similarly, the careers of top players were often judged solely by their performance at the Wimbledon Championships.

For George Hillyard, the All England Club was to be particularly important. He was initially a club member; he, his wife, and later his son, all competed in the Championships, and Hillyard's Olympic Gold Medal was won on the Worple Road centre court. From 1907 Hillyard occupied the position of Secretary. The club provided the background to much of Hillyard's life, and so the first years of its existence are worth exploring.

Some of the best insights into the early days of the All England Club can be found in Hillyard's own book, Forty Years of First-Class Tennis, in a chapter titled 'The Story of The All England Club' written by friend and chairman, Herbert Wilberforce.

Wilberforce relates that the club was not always the staid institution it later became. A wonderful committee minute in the first tournament year, 1877, records: 'During the winter months several meetings to transact business of little importance were held but, Mr Jones having mislaid the minute book, no record was kept.' Another minute, during the Championships of 1889, notes in the same spirit: 'The committee, having selected the best seats in the grandstand for themselves and their friends, adjourned.'

From the early days of the club some members were asking to play on Sundays, a proposal frowned upon in some quarters because of Christian principles of observing the Sabbath. In 1888 a poll was taken and the members voted two to one in favour of Sunday play. It is the experience of every tennis club since then that whatever the committee decide there will then be found neighbours who object, and so it was in 1889 that neighbours complained about Sunday play. The eloquent response of the committee was a resolution which stated they '*declined to sacrifice the convenience of the members to the Sabbatarian prejudices of adjoining occupiers.*'

Wilberforce also writes that in 1880 'The committee was strengthened by Sir Victor Brooke, a sportsman in many lands, *especially admired on the courts for the variety of his vocabulary.*' One can recognise a stock tennis club character of any era. Excellent! As an historical footnote, it might be added that Sir Victor Brooke evidently enjoyed big game hunting, and his proposed book on antelopes remained unfinished on his death.

That same year Julian Marshall became Club Secretary. Marshall was an able real tennis player who had taken to lawn tennis with a passion. There does seem to be a certain kind of person who enjoys being in charge of a tennis club (or maybe any club). They work tirelessly, get things done, take on every duty possible and believe themselves indispensable. Often they are, but for some reason they find themselves not universally loved. They may be seen as a little officious, possibly a shade self-important. Most tennis clubs, at some time, will have such worthy people on their committee. By all accounts, Julian Marshall was just such a man.

A wonderful photograph from 'Fifty Years of Wimbledon' by Myers. This is the 1883 Wimbledon Challenge Final featuring the Renshaw brothers on the centre court at Worple Road, Wimbledon. Note the absence of tramlines and the large crowds packed around the court.

As is often the case, there was a hugely positive side to his contribution. When Marshall became Secretary the club was struggling to break even financially, and only a small profit from the newly created championships gave hope for the future. Under Marshall's stewardship the club entered a new era. Profits for the championships rose to £300 in 1880 and then £540 in 1881. The ground was finally purchased for £3,000, and it was Marshall who deserved much of the credit.

In the first week of the 1886 championships, a serious incident occurred, which would have been anathema to Hillyard given his love of perfect conditions. Herbert Chipp, an able and experienced competitor, discovered a number of clover flowers growing in the long grass on the baseline of the centre court during his match. Not surprisingly, Chipp was upset. He mentioned the clover, along with his indignation, to Herbert Lawford, another top player of the day who was destined to win the singles title the following year. Famous for his powerful forehand and never-say-die determination, Lawford sympathised greatly. Both he and Chipp were serious men with a genuine love for tennis; they didn't want to be playing on courts that had clover poking up amid the long and uneven grass.

Chipp was quoted in a letter to the papers: '*The true bound of the ball was the exception, the false bound the rule … there was enough grass on the court to furnish a goodly crop of hay … clover-heads were showing distinctly in all parts of the court … etc.*'

Lawford was also a committee member, and when his comments were quoted by Chipp, Julian Marshall became defensive and critical, not of the clover but of Lawford for expressing his view publicly. He was also editor of *Lawn Tennis Magazine* and castigated Chipp severely for daring to raise any complaint. Chipp having said 'the false bound was the rule,' Marshall referred to him in *Lawn Tennis*, in a manner considered extremely witty at the time, as 'the false bounder.'

Nevertheless, later in the tournament the grass was better trimmed. Marshall shortly afterwards took the positive step of employing a new groundsman (or gardener, as they were then called) named Thomas Coleman, who was to retain the position for many years. Years in which flowers were never again seen growing on the Worple Road Centre Court.

Two faded (but wonderful and unique!) photos from around 1900. On the left is a posed picture of competitors at a tournament. On the right are five top lady players relaxing outside the referee's office. On the left of this photo is an advert for Ayres tennis balls which were used at Wimbledon until Slazenger replaced them in 1902 in controversial circumstances.

A major problem now arose due to his treatment of the previous groundsman. Maybe it was the clover, maybe something more serious, but Marshall decided that the man was guilty of dishonesty. He therefore had him arrested and sent for trial, before informing the committee of his actions. Unfortunately for Marshall, the jury threw the case out and the ex-gardener sued the club, winning substantial damages. In the ensuing recriminations, Marshall abruptly discovered he had run out of friends on the committee and was asked to resign.

Around this time many tennis players, as well as the secretaries of other clubs in England began complaining about the power of the All England Club, which had evolved into the body solely responsible for the administration of the sport in England. George Hillyard was amongst their number. Naturally any talk of dispersing influence away from Wimbledon was unwelcome to Marshall.

Nick 'Pa' Lane Jackson was a sports-mad organiser, journalist and administrator, born in 1849. He wrote his autobiography in 1931 called 'Sporting Ways and Sporting Days,' in which he remembers the formation of the LTA from a personal viewpoint. He makes the assertion *'I was virtually the pioneer of the formation of the Lawn Tennis Association.'* Jackson was 82 at the time of writing and the claim was a gross exaggeration, but he had been there at the birth of the LTA, and his description of these events is interesting:

My view was that although the All England Club had done excellent service to the game and was looked upon as the M.C.C. of lawn-tennis, the difference between that game and cricket was so great that the time was ripe for a governing body. As a journalist, however, I felt that it would be injudicious to initiate such a proposal, so I persuaded an old friend, Major-General Bartlett, of the Exmouth Lawn Tennis Club, to do so at one of the meetings convened by the A.E.L.T.C. In spite of the fact that the General moved his resolution in a very half-hearted and apologetic speech, he got a good deal of support. However, the proposal was ultimately turned down.

The next step of importance was taken in November 1887, when a circular to convene a meeting to discuss the desirability of forming a lawn tennis association was issued, after consulting with me, by H.S. Scrivener, the President of Oxford University, and G.W. Hillyard, both of whom were rather 'up against' the A.E.L.T.C. The meeting was held in January 1888, and attracted a large and very representative gathering, over which Captain Hobbs, of the Northern Lawn Tennis Association, presided. The resolution in favour of forming a national association was strenuously opposed by Daniel Jones, Chairman of the A.E.L.T.C., but in spite of his objections the motion was carried by an overwhelming majority, and the Lawn Tennis Association came into being.

In 1887 Harry Scrivener was President of the Oxford University Tennis Club, and a 22-year old undergraduate. Hillyard was 23. Revolution often comes through the young, and this was the case with Scrivener and Hillyard. The two men were close friends who later won the British Covered Court Doubles Championships in 1890 and 1891. Scrivener's campaigning zeal was based mostly on a personal dislike of Julian Marshall. In his role as President, Scrivener had written to Marshall about the Varsity match and received an off-hand and dismissive reply. As a proud Oxford student, Scrivener took this badly. He resolved to put Wimbledon, and Marshall, in their place.

George Hillyard was equally involved with Scrivener in producing the circular letter that tested the waters. Armed with a large number of favourable replies, they organised the meeting in January 1888 which brought about the formation of The Lawn Tennis Association, wresting powers from Wimbledon. This could be seen as ironic, in that Hillyard himself later became Secretary of The All England Club and

Scrivener Referee of the championships. Although certainly historic, Hillyard's part may not have been wholly altruistic. He was Scrivener's close friend, and both he and Scrivener disliked the high-handed attitude of Julian Marshall. But Hillyard may have had another motive. Wimbledon had, by that time, been hosting the Ladies Singles championship for four years. The event made a good profit and attracted large, admiring crowds. There was some criticism in the Press, however, that women shouldn't have to compete in front of such appreciative galleries, but rather the event should be moved away to the seclusion of the provinces. It was felt that ladies of refinement should not be required to exert themselves athletically, and possibly glow, in front of people to whom they had not been formally introduced!

In Wallis Myer's book, 'The Complete Lawn Tennis Player', Scrivener is quoted as saying that Hillyard himself was opposed to Wimbledon's control of the ladies singles event. This quote is referred to by Tom Todd in his excellent book 'The Tennis Players' when he discusses attitudes to women's tennis in the 19th century. To modern eyes, it paints Hillyard in a negative light. Todd uses Myers' quote to describe Hillyard as being opposed to allowing ladies and mixed doubles to be played at major tournaments. But throughout his career, George Hillyard played mixed doubles with a variety of partners, and Myers' assertion is the only *original* one I found to suggest Hillyard might have felt any envy of his wife's prowess. It might be possible, newly married at the age of 22, and given the times they lived in, that he initially felt insecure seeing thousands of onlookers showing such admiration whilst watching his wife run about a tennis court. But, in truth, Blanche Hillyard competed at a number of tournaments on a large stage before, and many more during, their marriage. She played in finals across England and the Continent, and in later writing Hillyard was consistently generous in praise of his wife and her ability. If in 1887 there was some unease felt by a young, newly married man, it seems to have evaporated rapidly as he learnt to accept and admire the success of his wife through the years that followed.

This photo features 4 top male players from around 1905 – Laurie Doherty, Frank Riseley, Sidney Smith and Reggie Doherty. The man with the watch-chain is W H Collins, President of the LTA.

Collins featured in an early disaster for the LTA when he captained the Davis Cup team to face America in 1902 in a 2nd attempt at victory. The Dohertys were selected, and expected to play. The Irishman, Joshua Pym, was also taken – a great player in his day but by then sadly overweight and out of practice.

The Americans had a strong team and Collins underestimated them. He picked Pym and Reggie Doherty for the singles and relegated Laurie Doherty, the Wimbledon champion, to play doubles with his brother. Pym lost both matches and a defeat for an unwell Reggie in one singles won the Cup for America, 3-2.

Despite this debacle Collins (he was LTA President, after all!) remained captain for the match in 1903. This time he picked both Dohertys, even when Reggie was injured on the first day and had to concede. At 2-1 up on the final day the Dohertys proved a point, each bravely winning their singles rubber in a tight fifth set.

Of such stuff are heroes made!

Although Scrivener and Hillyard successfully distributed their original circular, the pair made a basic mistake when posting out invitations to the subsequent meeting; they forgot to invite anyone from the All England Club!

Scrivener recalled what happened: *Our circular brought a number of favourable replies and we accordingly decided to convene a meeting to discuss whether an association should be formed. We sent out a lot of invitations, but by some unfortunate accident, for which Hillyard blamed a housemaid and the housemaid undoubtedly blamed the cat, a good number of clubs we intended to invite did not get an invitation. I was only an undergraduate of 22 and I did not realise the value of checking lists, not only of what I did, but of others' work as well.*

The fateful meeting was held on January 26th 1888, at the Freemasons Tavern, Great Queen Street. Scrivener blamed his friend for failing to invite the All England Club, but whether the omission was intentional can't be known. Certainly Henry Jones, who turned up anyway without a formal invitation, tried to use this omission to scupper the meeting, but the motion to form an association was supported by two thirds of those in attendance.

A provisional committee was set up immediately, with Hillyard and Scrivener both on it, accompanied by a large number of tennis worthies of the time. Herbert Chipp, of clover fame, was voted Secretary – a position he held for seven years.

An excellent cartoon caricature of George Hillyard from *Lawn Tennis and Badminton* Magazine

Chipp was an interesting character who clearly absolutely loved tennis – he wrote a superb book, titled 'Lawn Tennis Recollections' in 1898. He was a tall, forbidding, bearded figure, who was also ambidextrous, swapping hands so as to avoid hitting backhands. Tactically, he was an all-out baseliner, almost never venturing to the net, to the extent that when he did hit a volley the crowd would sometimes cheer in ironic appreciation. It might be thought similarly ironic that he wrote of Blanche Hillyard (who was that year winning the Wimbledon Ladies singles title for the fifth of six occasions): *'Mrs Hillyard has been known to volley but only when she has found the ball on her racquet and no other course open to her.'* He continued: *'Her backhand, although safe, is comparatively tame – moreover it is of a rather elevated character. Her service is overhand, and possesses no great virtue. In smashing power she is absolutely deficient.'* Clearly Chipp was not a huge fan of women's tennis!

In 1889, to George Hillyard's great satisfaction, **The** Lawn Tennis Association was formed. At that time the British tennis community saw no need for a national prefix to be included, despite the United States Lawn Tennis Association having been in existence since 1881!

Hillyard was voted onto the original provisional LTA committee

Many years later in 1906, now a member of Leicester LTC, it was proposed he should be the Midlands representative on the LTA council. This proposal is confirmed below

As a footnote, whilst reading Fred Perry's autobiography I came across a story which graphically illustrates some prevailing social attitudes, both at Wimbledon and in society. It is of a similar stamp to the early attempts to discourage ladies playing in public, although it comes some 40 years later.

Perry is currently the last British man to win the Wimbledon singles title – a feat he managed three times in succession as well as leading the British Davis Cup team to four successive victories. Amazingly, in his time, he was not popular amongst some sections of British society as he was a man perceived as not coming from 'The Upper Classes.' In his reminiscence Perry describes having just won the Championships for the first time in 1934 against Jack Crawford. He remembers: *In those days there was no formal presentation of the championship trophy on court. You simply shook hands with your opponent, picked up your gear and walked back to the dressing room. I had beaten the Australian Jack Crawford, and I went for a long soak in the bath. Suddenly, out in the dressing room, I overheard the distinctive voice of Brame Hillyard, Club committee man, talking to Crawford. 'Congratulations,' said Hillyard. 'This was one day when the best man didn't win.' Hillyard had brought a bottle of champagne into the dressing room and given it to Jack, whom I had beaten in straight sets not half an hour before. I leapt from the tub, rushed out and, sure enough, found Crawford holding the bottle. True, I hadn't been quite forgotten: there, draped over the back of my seat, was the official acknowledgement of my championship, an honorary All England Club member's tie. Nobody said, 'Here's your tie, Fred. Welcome to the Club.' Nobody even said, 'Congratulations.' The tie was just dropped there for me to find when I came out of the bath. Instead of Fred J. Perry the champ, I felt like Fred J. Muggs the chump.*

Brame Hillyard's rather more sympathetic claim to fame arose in 1930 when he was the first man to wear shorts, rather than long trousers, in the Wimbledon tournament. But when first reading Perry's story I wondered whether Brame and George Hillyard could be the same person. It is a story of such ignorance that had they been, I think I might have struggled to write this biography. Fortunately, they are separate people and I can't find any close link between them apart from the surname. Better still, I recently came across a quote from Hillyard which showed he was actually a great admirer of Fred Perry. It is in an article from an Australian paper in February 1934, a few months *before* Perry won Wimbledon for the first time. It says:

Commander Hillyard, when celebrating his 70th birthday, told the "Evening News" that he had assisted in the organization of about 40 Wimbledon tennis tournaments.

He said that he could not single out any man as a champion outstanding above all others, but that Mlle. Suzanne Lenglen was the greatest, woman player of all time. Nevertheless, I have a list of the 14 Wimbledon immortals'.

Those in it are in chronological order; the Renshaw twins, Dr. Pim, the Doherty brothers, Brookes, Wilding, Tilden, Johnston, Borotra, Lacoste, Cochet, Vines, and Crawford.

I should like to add **Perry***, because of his magnificent performances after Wimbledon.*

Happily, just a few months later and after so many years waiting, George Hillyard would be proud to watch a British player finally regaining the Wimbledon title. He would also get his wish – to add Perry's name to his list of the 14 tennis 'immortals'.

8

HILLYARD AND PRINCE GEORGE – ROYALTY AT WIMBLEDON

The role of the British Monarchy in the 19th and early 20th century was still paramount in a society which was unrecognisably more deferential than today. It is difficult now to appreciate the importance of royal patronage in Victorian and Edwardian society. For individuals it could bring riches, fame and position. For Wimbledon, and the fledgling sport of lawn tennis, it offered much the same.

The royal seal of approval was achieved in 1907 through the connections of the newly-installed Wimbledon Club Secretary, George Hillyard. He invited his friend and shipmate of his youth, the Prince of Wales (later King George V) along to watch the Championships. Accompanied by his wife, Princess Mary, the Prince of Wales sat alongside Hillyard in the committee box on Saturday 29th June 1907, watching the Ladies Challenge Round, while the subtleties of the game were explained.

This was the first visit by British royalty, and coincided with Britain losing both the singles titles to overseas players. In the Men's singles Norman Brookes from Australia became the first player from outside the United Kingdom to take the crown. At the same time the American May Sutton beat Lambert Chambers in the Ladies singles. Fortunately, with encouragement from Hillyard, the royal couple maintained their interest in tennis and continued to appear at Wimbledon. In fact they were present again in 1934 when Fred Perry and Dorothy Round won back both titles for Britain.

During that first visit in 1907, the Prince accepted the position of President of the All England Club, and additionally presented a challenge trophy for the winner of the challenge round. On his accession to the throne in 1910, the new King George became Patron of the Club, instituting a tradition maintained by succeeding Monarchs to the present day.

When Wimbledon moved from its Worple Road site to the current one at Church Road, it was King George

Their Royal Highnesses Prince George and Princess Marina

*To commemorate the Wedding Gift presented to
Their Royal Highnesses by His Majesty's subjects,
amongst whom is included*

G. W. Hillyard

In 1934 Prince George, the Duke of Kent, fourth son of Hillyard's childhood friend, George V,
married Princess Marina of Greece.
As a loyal subject, Hillyard gave them a wedding present, and to the left is the royal note of appreciation.

who performed the opening ceremony, standing alongside Commander George Hillyard. At the 'Golden Jubilee' Wimbledon in 1926, the King's son Prince Albert (later King George VI and the subject of the film 'The King's Speech') competed in the Mens Doubles event, although he lost a little ignominiously in the first round and never entered again.

At Hillyard's last Wimbledon as Club Secretary, the King once more made a point of turning up to sit next to his old friend. The Queen came twice. Throughout that championship meeting the weather was perfect – a fitting, although some might say unusual, swan-song.

Although Hillyard was no longer Club Secretary for the 50th anniversary celebrations, it was he who stood at the King's side and announced the names at the historic parade of previous champions on the Centre Court. There is a photo from that year of the King sitting in the front row of the royal box, flanked on each side by dignitaries, whilst perched behind him is Hillyard, leaning forward in conversation.

In 1929 Prince George became President of the Club and, after he was killed in 1942, his widow the Duchess of Kent took on his duties. The present Duke of Kent then succeeded his mother as President in 1969.

The royal connection was absolutely essential to putting Wimbledon at the centre of the country's sporting life. It was due to George Hillyard's teenage years as shipmate to the royal brothers that this connection began and prospered in the way that it did. The face of Wimbledon today might have been very different without it.

9

HILLYARD, WIMBLEDON SECRETARY

eorge Hillyard accepted the position of Secretary at the All England Club In 1907, a post he was to hold, apart from a leave of absence though the war years, until the beginning of 1925.

That first year the champions were Norman Brookes and May Sutton - both previously guests at Thorpe Satchville. Hillyard would generally have enjoyed a close relationship with the players, particularly in the early years when he was still competing himself. Not that he ever considered himself retired; in 1920 Wallis Myers talked about the crush of people at Worple Road: *On the morning of the Patterson – Tilden match last July, having an engagement to play a private game with Commander Hillyard, yearning for a little exercise to relieve his secretarial cares, I had to pick my way over the bodies of those who, for several hours before and still to come, were waiting for the gates to open.*

The most enjoyable part of this quote is the image of George Hillyard, Club Secretary, finding time for a knock-up on the Wimbledon grass before one of the most important afternoons of his working year. But Myers also illustrates the problems then being experienced on finals day with enormous crowds wanting to get into the old ground.

At the beginning of his tenure, the All England Club was still based at Worple Road. It was a substantial ground in the context of the day, with ten grass courts in addition to the clubhouse, offices, walkways, a food area and some seating for spectators. The Centre Court in particular offered a large grandstand, but even then the club was not proving nearly large enough for the demands of the spectators.

Hillyard would have had a large number of responsibilities. It is sometimes forgotten that the All England Club is first and foremost a private members club. Its function is primarily to serve the needs and interests of its members throughout the year, not just for the few days of the Championships. In essence, Hillyard's principal job was to keep the members happy.

Worple Road – Wimbledon's home before 1922. The railway line was dirty and noisy, but what an iconic place, and what an iconic photograph from English Heritage! Nine courts surrounding the genuine centre court, and some meagre tea tents in the far right-hand corner with a larger one and some parking behind. On the courts, matches are in play. Wonderful!

Of course, one of the things the members wanted was a healthy balance sheet to keep their own fees low and the quality of the club high, and therefore the financial success of the Championships remained paramount. The facilities particularly, as in any tennis club, the condition of the courts, were also important. Previously this aspect of the club had sometimes been neglected, but Hillyard was an expert on tennis courts and immediately made their upkeep his especial concern. Regarding the Worple Road courts he took a daily, hands-on interest, ensuring that the best staff, equipment, fencing and seed were all in place to bring them up to the very highest quality. As a player who himself enjoyed perfect conditions he insisted on a higher standard of court maintenance than had previously been the norm. It was he who set the high bar of excellence and professionalism for the Wimbledon grounds which have remained the benchmark of the Championships ever since.

One aspect of the courts he couldn't change was their orientation. Ideally any outdoor court in Britain is laid north to south. This is to avoid the afternoon summer sun shining directly in the face of the players at one end. At Worple Road the centre court was unfortunately laid east to west, meaning that on a cloudless finals day it would be almost impossible to see the ball for half the time. This was made worse by the rule until 1890 that competitors should only change ends after every set so that in a five set match one unlucky player would inevitably be condemned to spending the entire final set squinting directly into the sun.

Hillyard's obsession with Wimbledon's grass was gently mocked in the June 1913 issue of Lawn Tennis and Badminton.

It said: 'We regret to hear that Mr G. W. Hillyard is suffering from shock due to his encountering a worm on the centre court one day last week. Our readers wish him a speedy recovery for 24th June.'

The magazine also enclosed this full page cartoon of him in a life or death struggle with a giant worm.

Hillyard was nautically exact when writing in his book: *What is the orientation of the courts at the New Wimbledon (Church Road)? The answer is N.N.W. and S.S.E. This is the best compass bearing for afternoon play at midsummer with British summer time in force. Quite apart from the sun, the light at the New Ground is much better in other respects, particularly for the volleyer. The backgrounds of the centre court are 14 feet high, against five feet and six feet six inches at the Old Ground. In consequence, one has a clear sight of the ball where formerly one was always losing it against the varied dress of the spectators.*

In 1910 Wimbledon purchased a motor roller for the courts – an important innovation but the beginning of the end for the Wimbledon horses, which had previously performed this function alongside the ground staff. In Hillyard's words: *The initial cost of such a roller is heavy, something in the neighbourhood of £250 to £300; but, on the other hand, they are very cheap to run and so well made that the repair cost is practically nil … My advice to all clubs is to get a motor roller if they can possibly run to it.*

Hillyard, as Club Secretary, always spoke at the AELTC championship dinner. A toast to his health would be offered by the President and Hillyard would then discuss the Championships and give his impressions of the year. There were so many speakers at the 1913 dinner, with so much to say, that the band didn't start to play until after midnight. In consequence a large number of guests went home having heard a great deal of talking but no music. Whether or not the singles champions waited around to have their opening dance together isn't recorded.

'The Lawn Tennis Alphabet', by H. J. Crowther-Smith, was published by Slazenger the following year. This was a book of rhyming couplets with a different letter of the alphabet on each page, facing a cartoon of the subject of the rhyme. So, for example:

A for the Allens – those big merry twins,

Examples of how well combined merit wins.

Not great poetry perhaps, but the facing cartoons are excellent. The one of the Allen twins features the backs of two rotund figures dressed exactly the same, a racquet in each right hand, facing a wall. The impression is that of a gent's lavatory.

There could have been many names starting with 'H', but Hillyard's term as Wimbledon Secretary is highlighted:

While Hillyard's in Office there's nought can go wrong;

During Wimbledon week he goes 'specially strong.

On the facing page is a cartoon of him in profile, racquet under his arm and towel in hand. Once again, not memorable verse, but an affectionate and original cartoon.

Frank Burrow became Tournament referee in 1919 and spoke of Hillyard's influence as Secretary on the first post-war Wimbledon: *Much of the success was due to Commander G. W. Hillyard RN, who until he vacated the office in 1925 was a tower of strength, both from his firm hand in control of the general working of the meeting, and his personal knowledge of the competitors.*

I came across this (scratched) photograph in Hillyard's private album. The venue is Church Road, Wimbledon and the queue stretches into the distance. The paper seller holds up the words "Lenglen v McKane", advertising a match between Kathleen McKane (better known as Kitty Godfree) and Suzanne Lenglen. They played the final in 1923, but a second round match in 1922. The size of the queue, and the photo's place in his album, makes it possible it is a photo from 1922, the inaugural year of Church Road, and the crowds are queuing for a full day rather than a final where the total crowd might be smaller. All the men and women in the crowd wear hats, a policeman sits astride a horse whilst another stands watching, hands on hips. Six men wander up the road on the left wearing tall sandwich boards strapped to their bodies. What a wonderful photo!

There was a constant demand for space and improvement, illustrated perfectly by a report in 1913 of the club acquiring two adjoining houses in Worple Road – numbers 108 and 110 – to be used for offices, dressing rooms and the provision of food. A stand around Centre Court was also rebuilt and enlarged. The prime motivation for moving to Church Road in 1922 was the appalling crush experienced at the smaller Worple Road ground. It is ironic therefore that *Lawn tennis and Badminton* magazine published photos in 1922 and 1923 of the Wimbledon crowds – looking even more packed and seething than before.

The difficulties at Worple Road meant that plans to move the ground were discussed from the start of his tenure, but the outbreak of war in 1914 put the subject on the back-burner for the duration. After the championship meeting of 1919, with the crowds returning and expanding, the decision to build a new ground was confirmed. It is my understanding that Hillyard was heavily involved in the search for, and selection of, the Church Road site, and then collaborated closely with the architect, Sir Stanley Peach. This is difficult to prove conclusively without access to the Club archives, but his record suggests that he would have been a prime mover in all aspects of 'new' Wimbledon.

In a later chapter I discuss Hillyard's 'retirement', during which he helped found and run what is now regarded as one of the most beautiful inland golf courses in England. At West Sussex Golf Club he worked for an investor's council (which he had helped recruit), and at Wimbledon he was responsible to a club committee, but in both instances he was allowed to operate with a degree of independence and flexibility which is only earned by competent and confident people who relish responsibility. He was a great 'man-manager', but add to this his connections with society and royalty (never mind with tennis 'royalty' - legendary figures like the Dohertys, the Renshaws, Wilding, Brookes, et al), and it becomes clear that his role at Wimbledon was much larger than a mere functionary working for a committee. He was the instigator - a purveyor of success and progress during his time as Club Secretary.

In 1920 the July issue of *Lawn Tennis and Badminton* stated: *Nor must we forget Commander G W Hillyard who is the right sort of man to have at the helm. His sonorous voice is to be heard everywhere and he is always on the spot.* The December issue that year reported on progress: *The hope that the New Wimbledon will be ready for next year's (1922) championship meeting is growing, and the latest bulletin issued by Commander Hillyard to the effect that if we have a reasonably open winter so that building operations may go on uninterrupted, all will be in readiness early in June.* Plans to use the Worple Road turf at Church Road were abandoned and: *It has been decided to leave the old ground in status quo, so that if the work on the new ground is delayed the old ground will still be there intact, and ready, if wanted, for the holding of the 1922 meeting.*

In the event the Church Road ground *was* ready in time, and the championships left Worple Road, never to return. The Worple Road site was sold in 1924 to Wimbledon High School for Girls for £4,000. An era had ended.

The opening day of the new Wimbledon in 1922 must have been one of mixed emotions. The weather was just dreadful, with heavy rain falling in a constant torrent soaking the newly laid grass pathways between and around the courts. Before long, thousands of milling spectators were marching up and down them, turning the pristine grass into a muddy bog of brown sludge. King George and Princess Mary were present. At 3.30pm on 26th June the King banged a gong in the Royal Box and declared the grounds open. The

Making the Draw for the Championships at the All England Club. _JUNE 1920._

At head of table—A. Sterry; from his left round the table—A. H. Trim, F. R. Burrow, E. R. Clarke, W. H. Collins, C. B. Watson, Commander G. W. Hillyard, H. Anthony Sabelli (standing), and Hamilton Price.

In 1920 the referee, F R Burrow, wears a hat indoors. Hillyard sits opposite, looking tanned.

conditions were so bad throughout the championships that the tournament ran over to the third Wednesday.

Despite the problems of weather, the 'new' Wimbledon was considered a huge success, with great credit given to the Club Secretary. From _Lawn Tennis and Badminton_ July 8, 1922: _Such trifling criticisms as one has heard in the course of a week redound to the credit of Commander Hillyard and his coadjutors. They worked wonders in having the ground ready at all, and in putting in all essential trimmings. When Commander Hillyard made an announcement through the megaphone on the opening day the audience recognised his great work by giving him a rousing ovation. In the absence of Royalty he would no doubt have been acclaimed in song: 'For he's a jolly good fellow.' He deserved to be. He will be immortalised in New Wimbledon._

This was rather an optimistic prediction, as there is currently no commemoration whatsoever of Hillyard at the Church Road site!

A good story from 1922. The opening match between A. Kingscote and L. Godfree was played on Centre Court. Each player naturally wanted to be the man who served the first ball at the new ground. Godfree won the toss and served, and Kingscote returned into the net. Godfree then rushed up to the net, grabbed the ball and stuffed it into his pocket before anyone else could claim it. Later Kingscote, who went on to win the match quite easily, admitted he might have returned the ball, but he wanted the first serve on the new ground to be a winner.

Like everyone of his generation, Hillyard had mixed feelings about the demise of the 'old' Wimbledon. He said: _The ground in Worple Road was so saturated with delightful associations and reminiscences. One has only to shut one's eyes to see on the old Centre Court, as on a moving picture, the great players and personalities of the past._ He then admits of the need for a move: _It is at least a tribute to the enormous popularity of the game that we are all so fond of and many of us have worked so hard for. The old ground was naturally far more homely and intimate but had its drawbacks from a player's point of view. The noise of the trains was deafening to people in the terrace bordering the railway_

1922 was the wettest ever Wimbledon with play extending to the 3rd Wednesday. Here the covers are on and the rain is sheeting down but the crowds remain seated and there is not an empty seat showing on Centre Court. Were they waiting for the rain to stop, or maybe for the King to declare the new Wimbledon open? It is yet another iconic photograph from the Hillyard family album

In 1912 Tony Wilding requested in writing that, as champion, he should play through from the 1st round at Wimbledon. Above he is wearing his favourite "Crusaders" blazer from Cambridge University..

Captain Anthony Wilding died in action during the First World War. He won Wimbledon four years in a row from 1910 to 1913. His movie-star looks and adventurous, though self-deprecating, personality made him a "star" beyond the narrow confines of tennis.

All these photos are from Hillyard's album. Hillyard stands ready to drive away whilst Wilding sits, arms crossed, in the sidecar. Wilding was a motorcycle enthusiast and most likely this machine would have belonged to him.

"Lacoste and Borotra" - their names on one of the boards on the right of this picture. It is a fascinating photo of the Church Road ground, again possibly from Wimbledon's inaugural year, 1922

… and the sun was right down the court in the afternoon.

The 'new' Wimbledon heralded more change than just the venue of the Championships. It also saw the demise of the old system of the champion standing out from the 'all-comers' draw until the challenge round. For the first time a champion had to enter the main draw like everyone else, and 'play though.' To the modern eyes this seems an obvious way of doing things, but tradition at Wimbledon was, then as now, a vital consideration and traditionalists were in favour of the status quo. Anthony Wilding had been one of the first champions to argue against this practice – in 1912 he requested in writing that he play through from the first round in the upcoming singles. Hillyard, who privately agreed with him, made a reply on behalf of the Wimbledon committee which was published in March of that year, regretfully declining. Wilding later died in the war, but his influence remained. In July 1921, in his capacity of Secretary of the AELTC, Hillyard sent a letter to every competitor '*asking their opinion on the holders playing through in the Championships with a view to assisting the Committee in considering the question.*' The result was strongly in favour, and as a result this system was instituted in 1922 and has remained in place ever since.

Hillyard would end his own autobiography with lines from Kipling. In 1923 he oversaw the installation of another Kipling quotation above the Centre Court entrance through which the players pass. It is still in place today:

'If you can meet with triumph and disaster

And treat these two imposters just the same.'

These were words that would have appealed particularly to him - a principle he had done his best to live up to but, like many of us, with varying degrees of success!

The big move did not see the end of construction. Number Two court was opened in 1923 and Number One court in 1924, but with the major works at Church Road completed to his satisfaction, Hillyard retired as Secretary the following year, before the 50th anniversary celebrations in 1926. He had overseen the move from Worple Road and was now content to take a back seat to his replacement, Dudley Larcombe.

The announcement was made, with an article titled 'Changes at Wimbledon' published the following week: *There are very few, if any, of the world's great players who, on their visits to Old Wimbledon, or the New, have not enjoyed a morning game with Commander Hillyard … his handsome figure must be the most familiar sight at the Championships meeting. It is now 18 years since he was made Secretary … and he has always discharged the duties of that yearly more onerous office to the satisfaction not only of the club itself, but to the innumerable overseas visitors to the headquarters of the game. More particularly his efforts have been devoted to the production and upkeep of the perfect grass court; and in this direction they have certainly been most successful. There can hardly be a blade of grass, on the old centre court or the new, which has not met with Hillyard's personal supervision … it is reassuring to know that he will still be in charge of his beloved courts, although he relinquishes, possibly without too keen regret, the office work of the club. He will also be the holder of a new office – Director of the Championships – which he will no doubt perform with the breezy bonhomie which has made him so familiar and popular a figure at Wimbledon for so many years past.*

The article also mentions Hillyard's war service. It says: *He rejoined the Navy on the outbreak of war being appointed Lt-Commander in 1914 and Commander in 1917, and put in some much-appreciated work (of which he will not speak) throughout the duration.*

As we have seen, Hillyard's relationship with Wimbledon had not always been so positive. There was the 1887 Hillyard/ Scrivener coup which began the process that transferred powers away from the All England Club to the Lawn Tennis Association. And, always a notoriously prickly performer on a tennis court, there was the 1899 falling out with the Wimbledon referee and subsequent scratching from the final of the Singles Plate.

In the event, however, neither controversy adversely affected his reputation. Eight years later the poacher turned gamekeeper as Wimbledon Club Secretary. It was an inspired choice – a top tennis player with friends in high places, a man of passion and confidence, used to working on his own initiative, who would continue to have a huge beneficial impact on both the club and the game of tennis throughout his time at The All England Club – an impact which resonates to the present day.

10

FORTY YEARS

George Hillyard published his only book, 'Forty Years of First Class Lawn Tennis' in 1924. He had reached sixty, and had a great deal to look back upon.

The book is dedicated to Admiral of the Fleet, The Viscount Jellicoe of Scapa G.C.B., O.M., G.C.V.O., LL.D. (an extremely impressive list of initials), *'to whose keenness and enthusiasm in furthering all forms of sports and games the officers and men of the Grand Fleet owe such a deep debt of gratitude'*. This is typical Hillyard – no mention of the Admiral's naval ability; rather the certainty that any leader who encourages his men to play sport must be made of 'the right stuff'.

A review of the book in the Evening Post on 19th July 1924 was gushing, in the way of the time. Ethel Larcombe was a close friend, and (as Ethel Thomson) Wimbledon singles champion in 1912. Larcombe's husband was Dudley Larcombe who succeeded Hillyard as Wimbledon Secretary. She wrote in the Daily Mail:

Lovers of lawn tennis—and nowadays who is not?—will welcome the publication of Commander Hillyard's memoirs. He calls his book 'Forty Years of First-class Lawn Tennis', but it is infinitely more than that. It is an appreciation of the game itself, a study of its growth and popularity, and a glowing tribute to the personalities of its greatest players.

She then describes some extremely mild comments (in the modern context) that Hillyard makes on the state of the game, and continues: *But Commander Hillyard's warnings and criticisms, although entirely merited, are tempered by his obvious sympathy and desire to help. His heart is in the game, and given to us in his book, and the most enjoyable chapters are those in which he tells his own reminiscences, with delightful anecdotes about all the great ones of the past forty years.*

The writer then gives her own views of tennis, and ends with a little more gush: *The spirit of the game is becoming a little submerged under modern conditions and tendencies, but Commander Hillyard's book, written in entire devotion to that spirit, should and will help to raise it again.*

This isn't a particularly critical review, it must be said. But on one point I agree – the most enjoyable chapters are those in which Hillyard takes time to reminisce.

A review on June 28th 1924 in *Lawn Tennis and Badminton* was equally positive: *'There is but one fault to be found with 'Forty Years of First-Class Lawn Tennis' by Commander G. W. Hillyard R.N. - that there is not enough of it!'*

G. W. HILLYARD.

It may, or may not, come as a surprise to know that I personally have more than a single copy of Hillyard's original book

To the left is the frontispiece of one – it has "Yours ever" and Hillyard's signature dated 1924.

Above are some notes on the inside cover of another copy – clearly Mrs Pickering who is mentioned in Hillyard's book, was the mother of Basil and the great grandmother of Simon. Excellent!

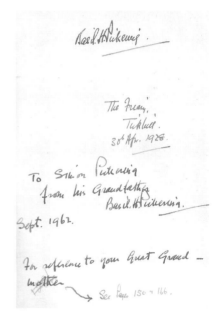

A recurring theme of the book is Hillyard's fondness for a bet. Whether golf, billiards, or a set of tennis, he was happy to put a wager on the outcome. He was also a man of strong opinions, who wasn't shy of sharing them with those around him.

Two betting stories concern Ernest Renshaw. Ernest was a famously consistent player, who as a result was able to offer large handicaps and still win. Hillyard was dining in the Riviera with an American, W. M. Cranston, who was criticising Renshaw's style of play. Hillyard defended his friend to the point that he made a substantial bet that Renshaw could concede a lead of 30-0 one game then 40-0 the next throughout a match, and still win. This was rash, as Cranston was a first–class player, and on being told of the bet, Renshaw was horrified. 'Fools and their money,' came to mind, but he promised to do his best, and the next morning met Cranston, on a calm sunless day on a perfect Cannes court.

Renshaw lost the first set nervously, 6-2. Odds of four and five to one were consequently offered, and Hillyard took the bets, more out of pride than hope. It was then that the match turned, and Renshaw won the next two sets for the loss of only two games. Given the handicap Hillyard says it was: 'the most wonderful exhibition of complete control of the tennis ball imaginable.'

His second story about Ernest Renshaw concerns a tennis party at which two top lady players were present. Renshaw had been giving them the same handicap as earlier he gave Cranston, with a similar result. Understandably the ladies placed the blame on their tennis clothing – at this time long sleeves, a starched collar, a tie, a hat, stays, and an ankle-length dress. The next day Renshaw borrowed the full set, and wearing his tennis flannels under the dress, still won.

Hillyard hit his first ever tennis ball before the inaugural Wimbledon tournament, and entered the Championships throughout much of its early history. His competitive career was long, successful and varied, giving him the opportunity to play against top players from different generations.

He lists some of the players he saw and competed against from 1880 through to 1924. After the Renshaws he discusses two baseliners – Herbert Lawford and Herbert Chipp, and then a succession of greats in Pim, Baddeley, Eaves, Mahoney, Lewis, and Gore. At its beginnings the game of tennis was disproportionately popular in Ireland, and Hillyard lists more than a dozen strong Irish players of that period whose standard rivalled the British. Much of the popularity of the game in Ireland revolved around the Fitzwilliam tournament in Dublin, run by the legendary Colonel Courtenay. His hospitality, and that of Dublin society, was famous.

Hillyard writes: *Open house in Fitzwilliam Square was the order of the days – and nights; and what with balls, dances and dinners, and hosts who would take no denial, it was indeed a difficult matter to do oneself justice on the courts the following morning. Everyone who was anyone in Ireland turned out at these meetings and the very jarveys of the jaunting-cars took a keen interest in the proceedings, and made bets amongst themselves over the railings of Fitzwilliam Square on the chances of their beloved 'Ghost' (W J Hamilton) against the invading Englishmen.*

An explanation of the above – evidently 'a jarvey of a jaunting-car' means the coachman of a one-horse carriage.

Ernest Renshaw was a famous case of someone who 'failed to do themselves justice the following morning.' So drunk after a night and early morning's entertainment, he found himself barely able to see the ball and lost ignominiously in a Fitzwilliam singles final.

Two Wimbledon champions at Thorpe Satchville. Left is May Sutton. Right is Norman Brookes, with house and spectators behind.

The next leap forward in standards came with the Doherty brothers. Between 1897 and 1906 they dominated tennis, and their own popularity cemented the popularity both of Wimbledon and the game itself. As mentioned earlier, the American doubles champions, Holcombe Ward and Dwight Davis, arrived for a visit in 1901. They were top-class players, and in Hillyard's opinion: 'rivalry of international character was the spark required to fire public enthusiasm more than ever…. from 1901, year by year, the game grew in public favour.'

Davis also donated the Davis Cup, inaugurated in 1900 with a match between England and America at Longwood, near Boston in the United States.

Another boost to popularity was provided in 1905 by the visit, already mentioned, of May Sutton, ladies champion of America, and Norman Brookes, men's champion of Australia. These foreign champions came by boat on long sea voyages which took weeks to complete. In their small way, these were epic journeys. Champions in their own country, they were setting out to conquer the world.

Here are the competitors in a Thorpe Satchville mixed doubles tournament in 1905, described in Hillyard's book, which he and Miss Pinckney won, Men stand behind their female partner. Wilding behind Miss Douglas, Brookes behind Blanche, Hillyard behind Miss Pinckney, and Reggie Doherty behind Miss Eastlake-Smith. Hillyard's friend, Eaves, has somehow appeared between Wilding and Brookes, and Gore and Miss Wilson have left early after losing both their matches. Having contrived to lose all 3 matches, despite partnering Reggie Doherty, Miss Eastlake-Smith looks rather dazed. Gwendoline Eastlake-Smith became Mrs Lamplough on her marriage, and was Hillyard's partner in his final tournament win in the Leicester mixed doubles in 1919. Miss Pinckney became Mrs Larcombe on her marriage and was Wimbledon singles champion in 1912.

The next great foreign player was the New Zealander, Anthony Wilding, who won Wimbledon in 1910 and again for the following three years. Brookes beat him in 1914 before war was declared. Hillyard tells a good story about the German player, Froitzheim, who reached the final of the All-Comers at Wimbledon that year but was taken prisoner shortly after the outbreak of war whilst travelling home from a Davis Cup match in America. Froitzheim wrote to Hillyard from 'somewhere in England,' requesting he use his influence to have him liberated *on the grounds that it was unsporting to keep him from fighting for his country.*

Hillyard wrote back that in the first place Froitzheim entirely overrated his influence, and second: *If I had any I should certainly use it to keep him particularly well-guarded until peace was declared on the grounds that lawn tennis players of his class were so exceedingly rare that we couldn't afford to lose one, even a German!*

Championship meetings at Wimbledon were resumed in 1919. Inevitably new stars came forward, particularly as Hillyard notes: *the appearance of the young French girl, shortly to become world-famous, Mlle Suzanne Lenglen … the crowds nearly broke down some of the stands in an effort to get a glimpse!*

The book's most memorable chapter, ironically, was not actually written by him. It was authored by H. W. Wilberforce with great humour, and recalls the early days of the All England Club. There has hardly been a book written since about the origins of lawn tennis that doesn't include excerpts from it.

Hillyard returns with a passage about suffering from poor umpiring decisions in which he says: '*I implore you, keep a stiff upper lip. Say nothing. Look nothing … it can be summed up in one word – control.*' There are so many stories elsewhere about Hillyard losing his temper when playing tennis that these might be seen as surprising sentiments!

Another chapter concerns Ladies tennis. Hillyard had asked his wife to write this for him and explains: *My path is indeed a thorny one. Worst of all, I've got to tackle the problem single-handed, as my wife utterly refuses to have anything to do with it. If the wife of one's bosom turns round on one in this manner, what will the others do!* He then complains that he could have written the chapter himself with his wife putting her name to it but: *my better half declined even this concession so I am left to bear the brunt. What a life! Women will do anything! Look at the suffragettes!*

This leads in to a story of suffragettes who were caught trying to burn down the Wimbledon stands during his time as Secretary. Then Hillyard settles down to a long and thoughtful history of the great lady players, from Maud Watson through to Suzanne Lenglen. He includes a generous appreciation of his wife's game, and finishes with a positive story about her as told by another player. It makes the chapter an affectionate one, so one assumes he must have forgiven her for refusing to write it.

There is a wonderful passage written by Major Cazalet, D.S.O. about a visit to Portugal.

Clement Haughton Langston Cazalet was a good friend and regular doubles partner of Hillyard. Cazalet relates that one day during the Championships he was watching a match on the centre court when a tall distinguished-looking man asked for the names of the players. The man then introduced himself as Pinto Basto, a representative of His Majesty the King of Portugal. Evidently the King wanted an English tennis team to visit Lisbon that autumn and to play in the tournament at Cascaes. Cazalet introduced Pinto Basto to the right people, and in short time a team was arranged featuring himself, the Hillyards, Mr and Mrs Durlacher, Mahoney, Eaves (the Doctor), and Miss Robb. The three ladies were expressly invited as the Portuguese were very keen on mixed doubles.

Cazalet tells how a letter was received saying a boat had been chartered to convey the whole party, and would sail from London docks on 4th October, just five days before they were due to play in Cascaes. As the members of the team had only been persuaded to take part on the promise of the shortest sea route and luxury train travel, this caused a difficult meeting. Cazalet smoothed down some strong feelings, and eventually everyone agreed it would be ungracious not to accept the use of a ship placed at their disposal.

This is Hillyard with Miss Violet Pinckney – together they won the private mixed doubles tournament described earlier. It looks like she also won a beagle!

Dorothea Lambert Chambers said: *'Miss Pinckney started a great work in 1908, organizing a ladies' volleying league, in which all ladies who entered a ladies' doubles event at any tournament were obliged to volley. A most successful experiment took place at the Beckenham tournament. Miss Pinckney and I played together at the Reading tournament, and although we were both base-liners, we determined to go to the net. We found at the end of the event (which we won, owing fifteen) that we had both much improved our volleying. Of course we made endless mistakes and were frequently in the wrong place, but it was experience so badly required.'*

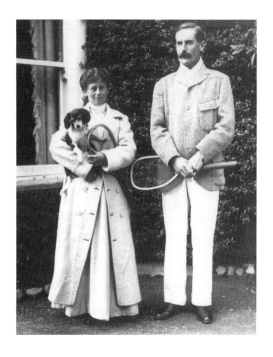

Found in the Hillyard album –this, evidently, is Mr Pinto Basto from Lisbon.

The writing below the photograph belongs to George Hillyard – Cazalet was approached by Pinto Basto at Wimbledon in 1901

Next, Cazalet was given the name of the ship and the London dock from which it would sail. Neither sounded promising, but he set off early so as to get on board and make things comfortable before the rest of the party appeared. The weather was terrible and getting worse when he arrived. After a great deal of searching, he finally discovered the steamer "The London" – *a regular tramp of about the worst kind, and not more than 1000 tons.* He shouted up to no effect. The only way to board was by a single plank: *down which dashed several No. 1 sized rats, scared by my approach.* He walked around the ship for quite a while, shouting, but no-one appeared. Eventually he discovered a glimmer of light leading down to a tiny saloon, lit by a smelly oil-lamp of the swinging variety.

By this time my temper was getting a trifle frayed, and I enquired with some asperity if he was the only man on board the blinking ship!

The steward said he was, and the crew would return in the morning. He and Cazalet then set about tidying the living quarters. While they were at work the steward told Cazalet that the voyage could take anything between six and fourteen days. In addition the ship had to make a diversion to Gravesend where they would pick up a large cargo of dynamite.

The party of tennis players then arrived at the dock gates. Cazalet continues: *To have any real appreciation of the scene that followed it is essential to have had the privilege of intimate personal acquaintance of each individual member of the team! To those of my readers less fortunate in this respect than myself, I fear it is quite beyond my poor powers to convey any adequate idea of its true merits. To begin with (and it may not be altogether unknown to some who read these lines) that not only my dear friend the Commander, but also Mrs Hillyard, have a marked gift for the most lucid expression of their views upon any subject or situation which appears to them to call for drastic comment! Then again, there was also Harold Mahoney, ex-champion not only of lawn tennis, but a present champion in his command of a weird and forceful vernacular peculiarly his own.*

Cazalet's plan was to get them into the warm saloon to discuss matters and then make sure their carriages left before the absence was noticed. This he did, and by the time it was agreed to return ashore there was no point. Cazalet then suggested they sleep on the ship and decide what to do in the morning.

In the morning the crew had returned and when Cazalet awoke at 8am: *to my intense relief I found, sure enough, the tugs had hold of us and it would not be many minutes before we should be clear of the docks and out in the stream.*

The party then met for breakfast. The bad news was that the ship would dock the next day at Gravesend to pick up a cargo of cordite and shells, and the Doctor (Eaves) refused to go any further. The good news was that the rest of the party agreed to make the best of it and travel on to Portugal.

At Gravesend the Doctor went ashore with a parting shot at Blanche Hillyard (presumably said in her husband's hearing): 'If you were *my* wife I wouldn't let you go.'

The weather was appalling and the sea rough. Cazalet then describes the journey in some detail. *Weather getting worse. George and Mrs Hillyard say their cabins are unbearable, and have taken up extremely cold and precarious positions on the on the two very narrow seats in the companion deck-house, and refuse all nourishment. Odd about George as he was never sick all his time in the Navy. Mahoney, having eaten the most enormous lunch, said he felt 'not disinclined to be ill.' He has now quite revived and has produced the largest hand camera I have ever seen. It looks like a small packing-case.*

The next day Cazalet describes ever worsening weather. Only he, Mahoney and the ship's captain eat breakfast. Commander George Hillyard RN doesn't make an appearance. Blanche says that many deaths at sea are from sea-sickness. Mahoney is washed into the scuppers a number of times whilst trying to photograph the sea. The camera fills with water and: *his language far surpasses anything I have yet heard.* Cazalet also notes: *His camera, when filled with sea water, is so heavy that even he can hardly lift it.* The steward brings a message to Mrs Hillyard that her maid wishes to inform her that she is dying. Blanche replies that she doesn't care as she's dying herself.

Finally the weather improves, and the whole party, bar the maid, returns to the deck. Late on Saturday 12th October, one week since boarding, they dock in Lisbon harbour.

From this moment, things improved. Two fast launches came dashing towards the ship with Mr Pinto Basso on board, full of apologies for their troubles. They were received by the chief of the Customs with great honour, and rushed through.

We were then escorted in torch-light procession to a saloon carriage drawn up in readiness, and half an hour later reached Cascaes, where a whole wing of the hotel adjoining the royal gardens had been reserved. Then followed a most cheery supper party, during which Pinto Basso explained the programme that had been arranged.

The next day they went to the sporting club and found it in perfect condition. In the mixed doubles tournament the Portuguese men partnered the English ladies, and the English men partnered the Portuguese ladies. King Carlos played with Mrs Hillyard but they lost to Cazalet and his partner in the second round. In the men's doubles Cazalet partnered the King, and they won the tournament, much to the King's pleasure. In the men's singles, George Hillyard beat Cazalet, then Mahoney in the final.

As important as the tennis were the social functions. A grand ball, where the Queen presented souvenirs to the team; a gala night at the opera; and a Portuguese bull fight (unlike a Spanish one the bulls were evidently not hurt). On the last day the visitors were taken to see the two palaces – one belonging to the King and one belonging to the Dowager Queen. Their driver was the King's brother. The next day they were homeward bound – *but this time on a much more comfortable vessel, which even the Doctor would have approved. So ended a most delightful tour.*

One souvenir given to Hillyard was a cigarette case in silver with coronet and flag in enamel on the back, presented by Phillip of Braganza. This is now in the possession of Jack Hillyard's step-daughter, Ada Dawnay. Luis Felipe was Prince Royal of Portugal and son of King Carlos. Both father and son were later gunned down in an assassination by two Portuguese revolutionaries in 1908.

Hillyard's book contains three consecutive chapters titled *Grass Courts, Hard Courts,* and *Covered Courts,* respectively, and concern one of his great obsessions – the search for a perfect tennis court. He begins by reminiscing a little sadly at the passing of Worple Road. It is the same tone used by Myers in his book celebrating 50 years at Wimbledon. Memories of Worple Road were memories of youth – of their finest tennis hours.

On the left, Miss Constance Wilson (later Mrs Luard) looking extremely smart
Above, it's the Doherty brothers again at Thorpe Satchville. Relaxed ready
positions were allowed having recently won the Davis Cup in America!

He talks again about players, with pencil sketches of the early tennis world and the characters that inhabited it. Amongst them are E. R. and C. G. Allen – the famous Allen twins. Many tennis books of the time refer to the Allens, although the brothers rarely played at Wimbledon. This was reputedly because the standard was always high and they preferred to expend as little effort as possible. The Allens liked to pick their tournaments, preferably venues where they had a good chance of reaching the final and winning valuable trophies. E.R. Allen played a good standard of singles, but as both brothers were a little overweight, and they were identical twins, they had their greatest successes at doubles. They were known as jokers and Hillyard says: *If at any tournament where they were playing you heard roars of laughter coming from the spectators, you could safely lay odds the Allens were engaged on that particular court.*

Hillyard mentions a tour of South Africa in 1908-1909 by a team from the All England Club, consisting of himself, Reggie Doherty, Eaves, and Lionel Enscombe. They played in 13 different towns. Ever the competitor, Hillyard gives the final statistics – 21 matches played; 16 won, 4 drawn, 1 lost. Hillyard spent his life playing tennis with people from different nations, and this was clearly something he valued. The final words in his book are about the Davis Cup: *In its 50 years or so of existence it has slowly but surely worked its way upwards and outwards, through prejudice and ignorance, until it has spread to all parts of the civilised world; and the greatest tribute that can be paid to it is the fact that in this year of grace 1924 there are no less than 23 nations challenging for the International Cup – America, the holders, making the 24th.*

Hillyard concludes his book with a quote from Rudyard Kipling:

For there is neither East nor West, border, nor breed, nor birth,

When two strong men come face to face, though they come from the ends of the earth.

11

THE OLYMPICS

The IV Olympiad of the modern era came to London in 1908. While most sports centred on the new White City stadium, the lawn tennis events were played on Wimbledon's Worple Road courts. Although a great fan of the Olympics in general, Hillyard was less enthused by the idea of tennis being a part of it. He puts this view strongly in his book:

As for lawn tennis in conjunction with the Olympic Games, the whole thing is an incongruous farce. You could as well have Olympic cricket or Olympic golf. It is difficult to believe that players or public can treat the matter seriously or care two straws about it. Why it is wanted, or tolerated, when we already have the Davis Cup, is beyond my comprehension.

I like this entry. But having read it, one might also ask why Hillyard entered the Olympic doubles in 1908 if he felt so strongly? Despite his misgivings there were a number of factors to persuade him. The event was at Wimbledon where he was recently installed as Club Secretary. The Olympics gave him the chance to represent his country. And possibly most important of all, they offered the opportunity of partnering his old friend and former Wimbledon champion, Reggie Doherty. Hillyard was also Honorary Manager of the Olympic tennis events and couldn't resist the chance to mix business with pleasure. The irony is that, due to the modern high profile of the Olympic Games as a brand, there are currently more references on the internet to George Hillyard as an Olympic Champion than to the rest of his tennis career put together. I wonder if he would have viewed this as 'an incongruous farce,' or perhaps it might have appealed to his dry sense of humour.

The London Olympics of 1908 are well documented in a wonderful book titled: '*The Fourth Olympiad BEING THE OFFICIAL REPORT, The Olympic Games of 1908, CELEBRATED IN LONDON Under the Patronage of His Most Gracious Majesty King Edward VII*', an extremely racy title, with italics and capital letters spread about like confetti, for a book which covers every sport in detail. It also contains an interesting photo of the Doubles final in play at the Worple Road centre court, with Hillyard and Reggie Doherty at the net against another British pair M. J. Ritchie and J. C. Parke. Hillyard hits a smash while his partner looks confidently on, racket down by his side. The stands are quite full facing the court, but relatively empty behind it. Most of the men in the crowd seem to be wearing flat-topped straw boaters against the July sun.

Two photos of Hillyard – same hat but next to a seated Mrs Lambert Chambers his moustache has become bushier.

The semi-final was a more remarkable match, played against another British pair, Clem Cazalet (one of Hillyard's favourite partners in previous years), and Charles Dixon. As noted previously, what constituted acceptable playing conditions was different to today. A small amount of rain may make grass courts slippery, and is now considered dangerous. In 1908 rain was only a minor inconvenience – spiked shoes were extracted from tennis bags, and play continued. It must have been a nightmare for the groundsman!

Club Secretary Hillyard would have had his doubts on finding his prized centre court abused by four men sliding about in spikes, particularly as he was one of them. For the first three sets of the five set semi-final, it rained constantly, and Hillyard played badly. Of course this was quite typical of Hillyard who preferred perfect conditions, and became fractious in adversity.

The first two sets went to Cazalet and Dixon 7-5, 6-2. Doherty won the third set, mostly on his own, 6-4, and after much complaining about the weather, the match was finally allowed to come off court. When play resumed, Hillyard and Doherty eventually went on to win 5-7, 2-6, 6-4, 17-15, 6-4.

The marvellous (and remarkably frank) contemporary account of the semi-final taken from the Official

Report repeats the above, but with more illumination:

In the semi-final of the Doubles, Dixon and Cazalet were beaten by Doherty and Hillyard. The first three sets were played in the rain. Somehow or other, Hillyard could do little right, whilst Cazalet and Dixon won the two sets comfortably. Doherty saved the third set by a superb effort when all seemed over, and then, with the players dripping wet, a successful appeal was made to the referee for an adjournment. There was some doubt as to whether the match would be resumed in the same evening, but, after a very long wait, the rain ceased, and the players again took the centre court. Very quickly Cazalet and Dixon went to 5/2 in the fourth set. It appeared to be any odds on them for the match, but once more Doherty was supreme in a crisis, and, although Hillyard improved, it was mainly due to the ex-champion that the match took a remarkable turn.

In a grim battle for that eighth game Dixon and Cazalet came within a stroke of the match no fewer than five times with Doherty serving! After this game after game went with the service, and at 15/40 Cazalet and Dixon twice more came within a stroke of the match. It was a heartbreaking experience for them; the more so as a sensational set ultimately went to Doherty and Hillyard by seventeen games to fifteen. Further disappointment was in store for Cazalet and Dixon, who assumed a lead of 3/0 in the fifth and deciding set, and were again unable to clinch matters. The small crowd waxed very enthusiastic as Doherty and Hillyard pulled up to 3 all, and then won the set at 6/4 and with it a remarkable match.

The final produced a match of uneven form, but it deservedly went to Doherty and Hillyard, the latter of whom, by his brilliant dash, made ample amends for his lapses in the semi-final. Although the match was won by three sets to love, it was finely fought out, all being 'vantage sets. Hillyard, so excellent later on, was not too good to begin with, whereas Parke and Ritchie opened in most promising style. Parke did quick things at the net, and met some of Hillyard's drives with an occasional stop-shot most brilliantly played. Ritchie was in the rear with his steadying influence and the pair went to 5/2 in capital style. The obvious duty of the opposition was to pass the active Parke, so Doherty, with the happy knack of rising to big occasions which characterised his play in all his matches, began to steer the ball most deftly over the Irishman's head and to pass him with some of the sweetest of backhand strokes. In this way four games were won off the reel, and, after Ritchie and Parke had led again at 7/6, Doherty and Hillyard won the set by 9/7. Parke, despite his rather erratic dash, played some fine strokes in the second set, during which Doherty occasionally wavered. Doherty and Hillyard won at 7/5, after being led by 4/2. Despite the rashness which led to mistakes, Parke continued to command attention in the third set, and won many aces with his swift service. The play proceeded on even lines—finally, 9/7 in favour of Doherty and Hillyard, who broke through Parke's service in the fifteenth game. Ritchie was not quite at his best, being uncertain in his length.

Hillyard was 44 years old when he won the Olympic Doubles. His partner Reggie Doherty, who had played so well and carried the pair through the semi-final, was 36. Reggie died just two years later in 1910.

In the men's singles, Hillyard conceded a walk-over in the 2nd round, as did his wife in the 2nd round of the ladies singles.

Remarkably, there was also an Olympics Covered court lawn tennis event, separate from the Grass courts, held in May at Queen's Club and also offering medals. In this, Hillyard partnered W. V. Eaves. Together they lost in the 2nd round to G. M. Simond and G. A. Caridia who afterwards progressed to the final. Once more there is a frank description of the match in the Official Report:

Hillyard began well, but ended badly, whilst Caridia was at his very worst at the beginning, giving no assistance whatever to his partner in the first two sets, and only playing slightly better in the last three. And: *In the fifth set Caridia was slightly better, though had it not been for Hillyard's inability to return the service at this stage of the match it must have gone the other way. Hillyard also served several double-faults, as many as three in one game, and Eaves lost his service when at 4 all.*

As a footnote, despite winning an Olympic gold medal, when Hillyard came to write his autobiography 18 years later, he never even mentioned it!

12

COURTS, AND EN-TOUT-CAS

*L*awn Tennis was given its name because, of course, it was originally played on lawns (despite Major Wingfield's early publicity suggesting it could also be played on ice, wearing skates!). Many national associations have, over the years, dropped the prefix 'Lawn' due to the variety of surfaces the game is now played on. For instance, what was originally the United States Lawn Tennis Association is now simply the United States Tennis Association. However, it can be argued that 'lawn tennis' is simply the name of the game, as opposed to other variations such as table tennis, paddle tennis, or real tennis. So the British Lawn Tennis Association may actually have the right idea, and clubs that dug up all their grass courts twenty years ago are still quite justified in calling themselves *Lawn* Tennis Clubs.

Throughout the 19th Century, lawn tennis in Britain was played almost exclusively on grass. Our climate cried out for an alternative, but most people treated tennis as simply a summer game, at its best when the sun shone.

Other countries sometimes had no choice, for instance where a hot climate made grass impractical, and so they experimented with a variety of surfaces. By the end of the 19th Century, different sorts of sand, tarmac, ash and concrete were all being tried in Britain. Playing indoors, it was wood which was generally the preferred surface, although it was often highly polished and suicidally fast.

Up until the turn of the century tennis courts were rarely built professionally. They were one-off affairs, which owners of a country house or club committees built for themselves, or simply an area of flat lawn marked out as a tennis court.

George Hillyard was to become a highly respected authority on the construction and upkeep of tennis courts and at his home in Thorpe Satchville he built what was often referred to at the time as 'the best grass court in England.' This still left him and his wife unable to play tennis much beyond the summer, and clearly this was unsatisfactory.

Meanwhile in Nottingham, Claude Brown was a struggling solicitor's clerk with a wealthy cousin. In 1902 the cousin acquired a bankrupt brickyard in Syston, a village just north of Leicester, and asked Claude to manage it. However, the bricks being produced were poor quality and there was a recession in the building industry which made business precarious. Fortunately for Claude Brown, he came across George Hillyard.

The first meeting of Brown and Hillyard is described in a company history and occurred in London. It records that in 1909 Brown met a gentleman called George Hillyard, then captain of the Great Britain tennis team and Secretary of the All England Tennis Club. Hillyard related a story of how he had been in South Africa playing tennis on courts made of crushed up ant heaps. On returning to Syston, Claude Brown took his unsold bricks, crushed them and with the resulting material laid his first tennis court at Commander Hillyard's country house in Leicestershire.

The Elms, Thorpe Satchville, around 1904
The site of the first court built by En-tout-cas

The original hard court at Thorpe Satchville was laid by October 1905. We know this from newspaper articles of the time reporting a tournament arranged by the Hillyards to celebrate its opening. This is referred to as an asphalt or tarmacadam court. It is vaguely possible that the company history has the dates wrong, and this was in fact the court built by Claude Brown. But it is more likely that Brown laid his own surface on top of the old asphalt, in 1909.

It would also seem possible that the original meeting was in Leicestershire, where they both lived, and much more likely that it was Hillyard who suggested the use of crushed brick for the court surface on discovering that Brown was in this industry. Certainly the dates coincide in another way – Hillyard's tour of South Africa took place in 1908/09.

Once the court was built, and enjoyed, Claude Brown's fortune was assured. Apart from Hillyard being the Secretary of the All England Club, he and his wife were, at that time, the most fashionable tennis couple in the world, hosting tennis parties for rich friends and top players. The firm acquired its name at one of these tennis parties. A guest, a fashionable French lady, showed off her new Parisian parasol which had been waterproofed and was called an 'en-tout-cas.' Claude Brown liked this description of something suitable for both sun and rain, and adopted the name for his company.

The author, on the lawn at Thorpe Satchville, where so many legendary tennis stars swung a racquet.

The author and Michael Charles, owner of 'Thorpe Satchville", at the site of the first en-tout-cas court

Word spread. The nearby Leicester Lawn Tennis Club where the Hillyards were prominent members was the first club to follow suit, having two courts built on its new Toller Road site in 1910, and the successful new surface was soon much in demand.

In 1912 the En-Tout-Cas brochure was headed 'Country House Work', and mentioned tennis courts in small letters underneath. By 1914 business was booming across England, and an agent had been appointed in the United States constructing new courts in large numbers. With the declaration of war, however, the tennis court business in Britain disappeared overnight. The company fell back on a large contract from the War Office to build folding tables and camp chairs, and also used space to stockpile wheat and flour from Australia and Canada. A few courts were still being built in America, but things were looking bleak until George Hillyard once again took a hand in the company's affairs.

According to the En-tout-cas company history, the Admiralty decided to construct tennis courts at their mainland bases *with the assistance and good offices of George Hillyard who was by then back in harness in the Royal Navy*. It also recalls that because of security problems the En-tout-cas foreman, George Steel, had to join the navy and even dress in bell bottoms.

Hillyard tells a story of building courts at this time, although he doesn't mention En-tout-cas. The date was early spring, 1916, at a naval station in the North of Scotland. Commander Hillyard was contacted by Capt. Lionel Halsey, RN and told that he must meet the Commander-in-Chief on board HMS Iron Duke. There he was appointed Officer Commanding the construction of a lawn tennis ground at Invergordon on the Firth of Forth for the officers of the Grand Fleet. The money had been donated by the head of a shipping line, Sir Charles Cayzer, in appreciation of the work being done by the Royal Navy in the war. Hillyard then describes the construction of hard courts at Invergordon, using all resources at his command.

Here is a photo from the Invergordon Archive. It says: "Jessie Millar and daughter on Castle Road, Invergordon. The old tennis courts are in the background. The date is around 1959."
Florence Urquhart told me that the Invergordon courts were finally dismantled in the 1960s by her husband's uncle, Willie Mackenzie. On the ground now is the Invergordon Social Club.
Florence also corrected Hillyard - Invergordon is on the Cromarty Firth, and not the Firth of Forth!

The courts were successfully laid to the highest specifications and still in use many years later.

In general I had little evidence concerning Hillyard's war service between 1914 and 1918, save that, like many people who saw combat, he didn't like to talk about it. Hillyard left the Navy with the rank of Commander. In his book when he describes the break from his normal war time duties to build the courts at Invergordon he says, revealingly: "It was all great fun, and very interesting, *and kept one from thinking of things which, at times, would hardly bear thinking of.*"

This photograph, featuring George Hillyard in naval uniform would at one time have belonged to his son, Jack.
The Battle of Jutland took place from May 31st to April 1st 1916. HMS Centurion was present at the battle.
It was a battle between the Royal Navy's Grand Fleet and Germany's High Seas Fleet. It was the largest naval battle in the Great War.
Fourteen British and eleven German ships were sunk with enormous loss of life. These deaths are the reason that the photograph is set over a black ribbon.

I then came across a photograph of him, in uniform, dated May 31st 1916. The name across the top of the frame is "HMS Centurion."

For those students of Naval History May 31st 1916 is a date of some renown, as it is the date of the Battle of Jutland. It would seem that, in a very full life, Hillyard was present at the most famous sea battle of the Great War.

In 1922 when the AELTC moved to Church Road, it was decided to build some hard courts to cater for the Club's playing membership as an alternative when the grass courts were unfit. In the event there were to be 13 grass and nine hard laid. With George Hillyard as Club Secretary there could be little doubt as to who would supply the hard courts – once again Claude Brown benefitted immensely from his close relationship with Hillyard so that in the 1925 Wimbledon programme he was able to take out a full page advertisement which read: *All hard courts at Championships Ground, Wimbledon, are En-tout-cas.*

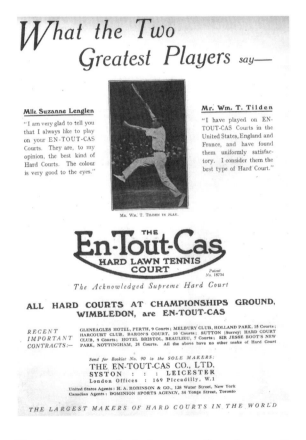

On the left, En-tous-cas advert in 1925 featuring the two Wimbledon champions.
Above, Hillyard's recommendation after the 1924 Junior Championships.
Note the company is now 'By appointment to H.M the King' presumably due to a recommendation to King George V from his friend George Hillyard.

The advertisement includes quotes from Suzanne Lenglen and Bill Tilden, the then Wimbledon Champions. Lenglen says: *I am very glad to tell you that I always like to play on your En-tout-cas courts. They are, to my opinion, the best kind of hard courts. The colour is very good to the eyes.*

Mr Wm. T. Tilden (as written) says: *I have played on En-tout-cas courts in the United States, England and France, and have found them uniformly satisfactory, I consider them the best type of hard court.*

For the two reigning Wimbledon champions to recommend any product would have had enormous commercial value. Both Tilden, and particularly Lenglen, were superstars of the day with major public profiles stretching far beyond the confines of tennis. Almost certainly Brown would have recompensed them financially for their recommendations.

The advert also lists London offices for En-tout-cas in Piccadilly, and overseas agents with addresses in New York and Toronto. Important contracts which get a mention include 15 courts in Holland Park, and 28 courts at Sir Jesse Boot's New Park in Nottingham.

For many years the British Junior Championships were played on Wimbledon's red en-tout-cas shale courts (I played there in them myself, as well as in Schools Wimbledon and the finals of the London Parks). Little did I know that the original surface had been chosen by George Hillyard in 1922. There is a wonderful photograph in *Lawn Tennis and Badminton* of all the competitors in the Junior Championships in September 1924 posing in front of the South East Hall at Wimbledon. George Hillyard is one of many dignitaries sitting in the front row. How inspirational for all the juniors of that time (and my time) to have the opportunity to play the National Championships at such a venue. With En-tout-cas never missing an advertising trick, the January 1925 edition then had an advert which said: *Commander G. W. Hillyard, R. N., Secretary of the All England Tennis Club, Wimbledon, writes: 'It may interest you to know that the nine En-tout-cas courts of this club upon which the Junior Championships were played last week gave the greatest satisfaction to the competitors who took part in the Meeting. On all sides I heard nothing but praise for them, from winners and losers alike. This is surely the acid test of quality.'*

The British Junior Championships at Wimbledon, 1924 - played on En-tout-cas.

In his book 'The Art of Lawn Tennis' written in 1920, Bill Tilden described En-tout-cas as the most popular hard court in England. After the First War the company continued to go from strength to strength, building courts across the country and beyond, becoming one of the world's foremost tennis court constructors, until finally ceasing trading in 1996. Throughout its 84 year life, the company remained a hugely important player in the development and provision of court surfaces – all originating from a conversation between George Hillyard and Claude Brown, more than a hundred years ago.

My absolutely favourite tennis book is '*Lawn Tennis at Home and Abroad,*' edited by A Wallis Myers, published in 1903. For the tennis buff it is 322 pages of absolute genius.

I mentioned this book to Alan Little, Honorary Librarian at the Wimbledon tennis library. Alan said that in his opinion it is the greatest tennis book of all time. And who am I to argue!

Myers gave a number of tennis celebrities the opportunity to make contributions. Harold Mahoney talks about 'The Old School and the New.' H. S. Scrivener gives his memories of tournaments, and those who played them. Mrs Stery has a chapter 'Lawn Tennis for Ladies'. Myers himself contributes a chapter 'Players of the Present'. Other writers cover tennis around the world – in Europe, Australasia, and America. Amongst all these reminiscences are photographs on nearly every page - literally hundreds. It is an iconic early tennis book written only 26 years after the first Championships at Wimbledon, and George Hillyard has a chapter all to himself, titled 'Courts and Conditions'.

In his first paragraph, he returns to a common theme: *It must be fairly obvious to anyone who gives the matter consideration that lawn tennis is a game requiring nearly perfect conditions to bring out its best points.*

Admittedly playing conditions at tournaments in 1903 were not perfect. But it seems possible that Hillyard's tennis might have suffered more than most from any imperfections of the time!

Hillyard mentions: *This world of imperfect courts and faulty backgrounds … a large white tent carefully placed at the end of the principal court to the utter ruination of the light … stroke after stroke is missed because the player has lost sight of the ball against some lady's white dress … not a single big meeting in England where both the background and floor are both first-class … bad weather is neither more nor less than calamitous to lawn tennis. Wind or rain completely spoil the game, and rob it of all its science … etc.*

Hillyard gives solutions to the problems, and talks about different court surfaces. His favourite in England is grass, at least when it is of high quality. But perhaps best of all are those he calls the 'sand' courts of Western Europe, particularly at the Beau Site in Cannes: 'the Mecca of lawn tennis'. Evidently they were *discovered and pioneered by Renshaw and Lawford at the end of the seventies.* By the time of writing, in 1903, the French Riviera was the preferred foreign watering-hole of the British tennis elite.

Hillyard relates both the two Renshaw stories from his later biography, as well as the journey to play tennis with the King of Portugal, although in less detail. In fact the whole chapter is littered with asides and personal opinion as he drifts away from the subject in hand. He does return to it when talking about covered courts, and there is an interesting photograph of 'the last match on the old Hyde Park Court.' The Hyde Park court held a particular fondness for Hillyard. It was one of the first buildings made specifically for lawn tennis, and the home of the original British Covered Court Championships which he won twice with his friend, Scrivener. When the court was demolished to make way for development, the Covered Court Championships were moved to the Queen's Club. Hillyard describes the best indoor court in England as belonging to Lord Cavan, his neighbour when living in Wheathampstead – the entire roof was made of glass, making the light almost perfect in daytime.

Another iconic book written in the earliest years of the game is that of the Doherty brothers, published in 1903 - 'R. F. and H. L. Doherty on Lawn Tennis.' The Dohertys were by far the most famous players of their generation, and this book would have been widely read at the time. They were also good friends with George Hillyard, and it is no surprise that he was asked to contribute a chapter titled 'Some hints on the construction and care of grass courts.'

He starts with a familiar theme: *The paradise of a lawn tennis player would be a perfect English summer day; a well matched Double; and last by no means least, a really good grass court. This latter, even in this year of grace 1903, is so great a rarity that I verily believe the majority of people have never seen, much less played on one!*

Hillyard stresses the importance of a good background to the court, and a large amount of room at the side and ends. He discusses using turf, raising grass from seeds, drainage and watering, rolling, mowing, and general upkeep. This is written five years before his appointment as Secretary of the All England Club where he took day to day responsibility for maintaining and improving the quality of the courts. He clearly had a deep knowledge of the subject and a genuine interest – a perfect combination for his future role.

Mrs Lambert Chambers, who won the Wimbledon singles seven times, said: *There are hundreds of splendid golf greens and cricket pitches all over the country, but for some inexplicable reason a good grass lawn tennis court is, as Mr*

George Hillyard pictured at Dinard in France in 1905 with two close friends, and two great players. A relaxed Lambert Chambers, centre, and Norman Brookes

G.W. Hillyard remarked, 'almost as rare a sight as a dead donkey'. Happily we get this rare spectacle at Wimbledon under Mr. Hillyard's able care and management.

Towards the end of his stewardship at Wimbledon, Hillyard returned again to the subject of tennis courts in his autobiography, written in 1924. Now he was more expansive with, as mentioned earlier, three separate chapters titled Grass Courts, Hard Courts and Covered Courts. Or as he says more literately: *Courts, like All Gaul in Julius Caesar's time, may be divided into three parts.*

Hillyard covers many of the same points as in previous writing but in greater detail. To anyone interested in the production or maintenance of grass courts it remains hugely interesting. He again mentions surrounds as vitally important and speaks about the most suitable varieties of sapling. He particularly recommends that courts should be 'boxed in' to give them a separate feel, with surrounds made of high hedges, or walls covered in greenery. There is no doubt that in private houses this would have given the best playing conditions due to good background and shelter from the wind, as well as a wonderful aesthetic feel. Interestingly some of the larger grass court clubs of my youth would often have a handful of single courts separated in this way, as well as high hedges dividing banks of courts. The trend today in clubs is much more towards courts being in rows of two or three, with less separation except by simple fencing. This is more practical for a modern tennis club, but perhaps the early trend of at least one or two separate single courts was to do with the origins of tennis in the country houses – many of whose owners were the same people who founded and ran the clubs.

When speaking of hard courts, Hillyard mentions En-tout-cas, and says: *I think there is nothing yet discovered that is as good as burnt clay, which is practically the material out of which En-tout-cas courts are made.*

Hillyard finishes with some interesting conjecture in the context of today: *There are no perfect hard courts at present. But I am confident that one of these days some surface will be invented that is resilient, porous, and durable. The surface will give the same type of bound as fast grass, and will have neither the skid of too-polished wood nor the 'hang' of the ordinary hard court. There will be no expense of upkeep or renovation, as no watering, rolling. No top-dressing or marking out will be required, for the lines will be part of the surface permanently let in. The colour will be dark green – the ideal colour for sighting the ball. Although the cost of such a court may be high, in reality it will be an economy, as not only will there be no charge for upkeep, but balls, rackets, and shoes will last far longer for there will be no gritty surface to cut them; and, which is equally important, the strain and jar on one's feet and legs will be reduced to a minimum. If this dream comes true it will probably revolutionise lawn tennis, and may, in time, do away with grass courts altogether.*

Considering this was written in 1924 it is remarkably prescient. Sand covered carpet courts began appearing in British tennis clubs in the 1980s, mostly to replace the more labour intensive surfaces of grass and shale. They were generally green, and claimed almost every attribute that Hillyard mentions in his prediction, and as a result became the most popular surface in British tennis clubs.

Improved technology has continued to make the playability of this surface marginally better, although the current preference, particularly amongst performance coaches and stronger players, is towards slower, higher bouncing surfaces. But the fact remains that in 2012 amongst general club members the green artificial-grass sand-filled carpet court remains extremely popular and amazingly similar to Hillyard's ideal surface, predicted some 60 years before its invention.

13

HILLYARD AS UMPIRE

As noted earlier, George Hillyard umpired as well as played. In fact he was acknowledged as one of the top tennis umpires of his day, and was regularly in the chair for the Wimbledon Ladies final. Undoubtedly he would have been helped in this by his position as Secretary of the All England Club, but equally he possessed an authority in the game ideally suited for the role of umpire.

It is recorded that Hillyard umpired every Wimbledon Ladies final from 1919 to 1932. It is likely he also umpired some between 1908 and 1914, but there seems no definite record for this period.

In 'Twenty years of Lawn Tennis,' published in 1921, Wallis Myers refers to the best British umpires, and cites Commander George Hillyard first. One can imagine that his tall and commanding figure would have added a touch of quality to the finals of any suburban tournament! In Europe it was British umpires, mostly from the Officer class, who were much in demand for their confident and patrician attitude from the chair. This said, it is undoubtedly true that at that time the Americans were ahead in terms of the organisation and training of officials, and it was not until 7th August 1919 that the formation of a National Umpire's Association was announced in Britain.

In the Wimbledon Ladies Final of 1922, the first at the 'new' Wimbledon, Suzanne Lenglen beat Mrs Mallory. Hillyard was umpire, as *Lawn tennis and Badminton* reported: *The presence of Commander Hillyard in the umpires chair always seems to be a moral support for Mlle Lenglen. He would be the umpire of her choice if players had any choice in the appointment of umpires which, of course, they have not. His personality and prestige demand the very best that players and linesmen can give. They are always on their mettle.*

In 1926 what was billed as the most keenly anticipated match of all time was to take place at the Carlton Club in Cannes. Suzanne Lenglen had completely dominated the world game since 1919 when she won

The great Suzanne Lenglen in action at Wimbledon in a photograph from Hillyard's private album.
Hillyard was reputedly her favourite umpire.
For his part, Hillyard considered Lenglen the greatest female player of all time

her first Wimbledon title. Helen Wills at 20 was the American champion, and she bravely travelled to France hoping to engineer a match against the champion in her own backyard. Initially odds of 10-1 were offered in favour of Lenglen, but these shortened as it became clear she was avoiding a confrontation with Wills. The longer events were delayed the more the pressure mounted, and eventually a confrontation became inevitable.

As it turned out, this match was to be the one and only singles encounter between the two. It took place on Tuesday, 16th February 1926. Heavy rain from the Tuesday to the Thursday of the previous week meant that the tournament was prolonged, but the weather appeared perfect for the final. 'The greatest match of all time' naturally required the most respected umpire - and this was George Hillyard. His linesmen were Cyril Tolley, an amateur golf champion; Clem Cazalet, Hillyard's sometime doubles partner; Roman Januch, the professional at the Cannes Tennis Club; and Lord Charles Hope. Guests included ex-King Manuel of Portugal; Grand Duke Michael of Russia; Prince George of Greece; the Rajah of Pudakota; the Duke of Westminster; the Duke of Connaught; Baron de Graffenried; and Count de Bourbel. The stands were absolutely packed and the watching crowd barely contained from spilling onto the court surface.

The match began just after 11 in the morning. Suzanne Lenglen won the first set 6-3. At 6-5, 40-15 to Lenglen in the second set, Wills hit an apparent winner into a corner of the court but there was a loud cry of 'Out.' The players ran to the net to shake hands, and the crowd erupted onto the court to congratulate their local heroine. It was then that Lord Charles Hope approached the chair through a mass of people to tell Hillyard that he hadn't called the ball out. The shout had come from the crowd.

Hillyard, unflustered, called the score 40-30 and ordered that the match be continued. After a few minutes confusion the court was finally cleared and, noticeably affected by what had happened, Lenglen lost the next three points to put the score back to six-all. Fortunately for her she recovered to win the next two games, and the match, leaving Hillyard to call the score at 6-3, 8-6 to the Frenchwoman.

Hillyard, as an umpire and in life, was a man of definite and strong opinions, which is possibly why he became the victim of a practical joke at the Leicester Tournament one year. He was competing in a men's doubles match before a small gallery when a telegram was suddenly brought to the courtside and Hillyard's name called. Could it be bad news? Everything stopped as Hillyard rushed over to the bearer and ripped open the telegram. He read the words written there, then without a word marched across and removed the singles sticks supporting the net. They had been wrongly left in place at the start of play and a watching fellow-competitor having spotted the error had sent him a telegram to point it out.

14

CRICKET

Throughout his days in the navy, George Hillyard played a variety of sports, but the particular interest of his youth was cricket - 'Cricket for us – every time and all the time.'

Hillyard was a right-handed batsman, and right-arm fast-medium bowler. He played cricket as a young boy, and a more intense period of regular practice and some coaching followed when training on HMS Britannia between the ages of 13 and 15. During his time there, Hillyard was captain of the cricket team for two years.

Soon after leaving the Navy in 1886, he made a successful appearance for Middlesex Colts against M.C.C. at Lords, taking six wickets for 13 runs, as well as scoring 21 himself. As a result he was invited to play for the senior Middlesex County side. After a short run in the team he became disillusioned, and from 1887 until 1890 virtually retired from the first-class game with only a single representative match in 1887 for the South against the North. Hillyard later placed the blame on the hard county wickets that bruised his heel and made fast bowling difficult. He also observed that his time in the Navy after Britannia had made it impossible to gain the required amount of practice to play at such a high level.

By the start of the summer of 1891, Hillyard hadn't taken part in a first class game for four years. He subsequently played four first class matches in May and June of that year– two for M.C.C., one for the Gentlemen Players, and one for a team called AJ Webbe's XI against Cambridge University. He followed this with some matches for Hertfordshire (he was living in Wheathampstead at the time).

As observed earlier, throughout his life George Hillyard had a 'face that fits'. So when a cricket tour of America was proposed in 1891, it can be little surprise that Hillyard was invited to take part, despite the fact that he had hardly played seriously for some time and was out of practice. His sudden burst of activity that summer was an effort to remedy the situation, but purely on cricket form he might not have been selected. However, as a good conversationalist, a well-connected sportsman, and an upright member of any 'Gentlemen's' team, he was undoubtedly one of the first on the list.

Left: 'The Illustrated American' 1894

HILLYARD WAITING TO BAT

Right: cover of the 'Cricket Field' in July 1894. Inside is an appreciative article about George Hillyard

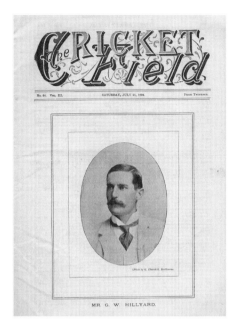

MR. G. W. HILLYARD.

The party of English cricketers which toured North America In the winter of 1891–92 was led by Lord Martin Hawke. The visitors had a total of eight matches scheduled; six in the United States and two in Canada including two first-class fixtures, both against the Gentlemen of Philadelphia.

Lord Hawke was a captain of Yorkshire and England, who also led touring parties to India, South Africa and the West Indies. Besides Hillyard, the party to America contained some popular characters in the game. Notable county cricketers Herbie Hewitt, Kingsmill Key, Charles Wright and Charles Wreford-Brown (also an England football captain) were on the tour, as were Viscount Throwley and Sammy Woods, one of only five cricketers to have represented both England and Australia.

The party left England in mid-September 1891. The crossing was difficult, with Herbie Hewett, George Ricketts and Charles Wreford-Brown particularly suffering from seasickness. On the fourth evening, Sammy Woods, who wasn't affected, tried to get the men to take dinner with him. He served champagne and vegetable soup, but an American who was also suffering commented 'Say steward, did you bring this up or did I?' None of Woods' team-mates managed to eat the dinner.

Hillyard played in both first-class matches in Philadelphia, with honours even, but he was unwell, batted down the order, and bowled little more than a handful of overs in each innings. After these two early matches, the rest of the tour was less competitive and the English team was rarely troubled. Off the field, things were very much to the liking of the tourists who were impressed by American hospitality, with large crowds following the English cricketers wherever they went.

Lord Hawke returned to America in 1894, having toured Ceylon and India the previous year. The team contained just three players from the 1891 visit, including Hillyard. This was a much shorter tour - only four matches, with the visitors this time winning both their first class games against Philadelphia. Hillyard contributed more to the team's successes in these matches than previously, taking three wickets in the first innings.

The New York Times reported on September 22nd 1894 that 10,000 spectators watched the match in Philadelphia. It also says (perhaps reflecting the priorities of the American cricket follower): *Warm weather allowed the ladies to don their prettiest gowns. Philadelphia society attended the match and the numerous coaching parties gave the field a gala appearance.*

By October 10th, the New York Times reported the tour as over, with Hillyard and six other players on their way to New York and then England, while Lord Hawke and C. W. Wright headed for the West Indies on a pleasure trip. Two more were going deer shooting in Canada. The Times also notes that *Lady Agnes de Trafford and Miss de Trafford will spend some time sightseeing in the United States, making their first stop at Newport,* recounting the minutiae of celebrity life in a manner not unlike the fanzines of today.

THE ENGLISH TEAM.

1. L. C. V. Bathurst.   2. W. F. Whitewell.   3. R. S. Lucas.   4. G. J. Mordaunt.   5. A. J. L. Hill.   6. G. W. Hillyard.   7. J. S. Robinson.
8. Kenneth McAlpine.   9. G. R. Bardswell.   10. C. W. Wright.   11. Lord Hawke.   12. Lady Agnes.   13. Miss de Trafford.   14. C. E. de Trafford.

'The Illustrated American' 1894. Lord Hawke's cricket team in America. Hillyard smiling, possibly because he's managed to leave off his blazer for a bet!

The Illustrated American magazine reported on both tours in some detail, with photos of the teams. In 1894 they admitted: *The game of cricket to the uninitiated is rather perplexing. It is hard to understand why it is so long drawn out, or why the players go about it in a sure, slow, deliberate manner and take so few risks in running between wickets. There is not enough slap and dash about it to please the average American. Despite this, the ground was full of paying spectators and the great stand and the benches about the field were occupied by well-dressed men.*

The New York Times in September 1894 produced cartoon drawings of some of the principal English tourists alongside short biographies. These included Hillyard, of whom it was said: *G. W. Hillyard should prove one of the principal bowlers of the current team, for he has been doing splendid work this season in England, and only two weeks ago he secured five wickets for 18 runs against Surrey's powerful batting aggregation.*

On July 21st 1894 a magazine called 'The Cricket Field' published an excellent article titled 'Chats on The Cricket Field.' The subject was Mr G. W. Hillyard, who was then 30 years old. After a short introduction it says: *For a bowler whose early years were passed without any adequate practice he has shown really wonderful progress – such progress that every lover of cricket must regret that he was ever led away from the paths of rectitude to play lawn tennis. Moreover there can be little doubt, to a cricketer at any rate, that nature gave him his long reach for the express purpose of bowling other people out, and not, as tennis players assert, with the object of enabling him to stop passing shots.*

Hillyard is asked whether he likes tennis better than cricket. He gives a long and revealing answer: *This is a remarkably difficult question because the two games are so different. Many people think that lawn tennis is an easy game, and so it may be, in ordinary practice. But when it comes to a five-set match it is quite a different thing. One often plays a dozen sets in an afternoon against good men, and works as hard as possible for the whole time without feeling any fatigue, but the strain which is put upon one in a match is enormous. You must go on; there is no chance of a rest as there is in cricket; you have no captain you can ask to take you off for a set or two; you must go on and on, even if the match lasts two or three hours; there is no stopping for rain, and you must never for an instant take your eyes off the ball. Not that there is no hard work at cricket – far from it. But my meaning is that because a man plays lawn tennis he may not necessarily be afraid of hard work. It nevertheless seems to me that lawn tennis is not really a game suited to our climate. It ought to be played under perfect conditions of weather and wind and turf. In England it is very seldom that you get these conditions, except on a covered court. For though your turf may be as perfect as turf can be, it is too frequently affected by rain. The South of France is the place for the game. On the other hand, cricket suits our climate exactly, and there are moments which are exquisite, even when the rain and the wind and the turf have all done their worst – even if you are a bowler. Take today, for instance. How jolly it would be to be playing at the Oval on a sticky wicket, instead of having to play at Wimbledon on a sticky court. But my partner extracted a promise from me to play with him in the Doubles long before the county fixtures had been arranged.*

Hillyard talks about the (negative!) influence of tennis on his batting, and is then asked where his early cricket was played. He replies: *Chiefly at Dartmouth, during my time on the Britannia. We were sent ashore around four o'clock and made to practice in the nets. Twice a week we had matches. As a matter of fact, we got more cricket than most boys … we had a strong eleven, and in the last year, during my captaincy, it is said to have been the strongest that ever represented the Britannia … before my Britannia days, when I was eight or nine, an opportunity was given me of seeing Surrey play at the Oval, and there is a distinct picture in my mind of Street bowling and Pooley keeping wicket. It all seemed to me very wonderful, and an immediate longing to take part in first-class cricket took possession of me. But after my period on the Britannia was over, half a dozen years at sea followed, and of course there was no opportunity to practice.*

George Hillyard's son, Jack (above front right outside an unnamed cricket pavilion), was an all-round sportsman like his father. On the left is the scorecard from the famous "Fowler's match", in 1910. The match is named after the captain of Eton College, Robert Fowler, whose outstanding batting and bowling performance allowed Eton to win by 9 runs after Harrow School asked Eton to follow on 165 runs in arrears. *Wisden* stated: 'In the whole history of cricket, there has been nothing more sensational'. Jack himself scored 62 runs in the 1st innings, was bowled by Fowler for a duck in the 2nd, then took Fowler's wicket in the 2nd innings.

When asked if he played cricket at all whilst serving on HMS Bacchante, he describes matches in Fiji, the West Indies, the Cape, Colombo and Singapore. On his return to England he played again at the Naval College, but his main club was Chiswick Park: *In those days my batting was much better than my bowling, so much so that in my last year for the Park my average was over 50, thanks to several hundreds.*

At the time of the interview Hillyard was clearly still enjoying his cricket and was playing for Leicestershire, through a residential qualification. That year there was also a large full-page photograph of him in the magazine 'Famous Cricketers and Cricket Grounds.' A small accompanying article says: *Though perhaps at one time better known as a lawn tennis player, G W Hillyard has during the last few years fairly established his right to a prominent position among the amateur cricketers of the day … His height has been of use to him, both as a batsman and a bowler. Though a fairly reliable run-getter, his reputation has mostly been made by his bowling. With an easy delivery, well over head, he is above medium pace, getting up very quickly from the pitch.*

By 1894, Hillyard was fully back in harness, with three busy seasons for Leicestershire in which he regained his enthusiasm and his form. Because of tennis and other commitments, as well as the thinness of the fixture list compared with today, he only played 49 first class matches in his on-and-off ten year cricket career to 1896. He was not a particularly accomplished batsman at this level, with a first-class career average of just 9.18. As a bowler he was more successful, taking 145 first-class wickets for an average 21.67 runs.

Well after the end of his playing career, Hillyard called his book 'Forty Years of First Class Tennis' – adopting the language of cricket to describe the tennis world of which he became such a part. In that book he only mentions cricket in passing. In one instance he illustrates the importance of watching the ball at all times in tennis with a story from the game of cricket.

I remember once when playing Derbyshire at cricket, having a yarn in the luncheon hour with that fine all-round professional, Chatterton.

'Prince Ranjitsinhji, sir? Of course, sir. Most difficult man to get out in England.'

When I asked why, Chatterton replied: 'Because he watches the ball further onto the bat than anyone else.'

He turned to his pal Davidson who was listening, and said: 'That's so, isn't it George?'

Davidson nodded assent.

Now, those two Derbyshire professionals knew what they were talking about. Therefore watch the ball at lawn tennis, and as far onto the racquet as you can.

This extract is interesting for more than the advice on offer. There is also the light cast on the class system when the cricket 'professional' uses 'sir' twice in speaking to 'gentleman' Hillyard. Set alongside this is the obvious respect that Hillyard has for the cricketer's knowledge and skill, as well as his acknowledgement of it by recording the conversation. In fact, it's quite an affectionate passage, but very much of its time.

Hillyard's last first-class cricket match was in 1896. He was thirty-two years of age. Cricket had been the game of his youth, the game he instinctively loved, and certainly he valued the opportunities for play and friendship that it offered. He always loved conversation with friends and other sportsmen. He loved to 'yarn'. But arriving at Thorpe Satchville he entered another stage of his life. He shortly came to leave cricket behind, and moved on to other sports. Thorpe Satchville did offer great opportunities for these – the billiards room, shooting in the surrounding countryside, the private nine-hole golf course, and the opportunity to ride to hounds with The Quorn Hunt and others. 'Boys with toys' might be an apt modern description. But most of all, it was now tennis that took centre stage. Hillyard approached playing first-class tennis with the same enthusiasm he had previously applied to first-class cricket.

15

BLANCHE

No story of George Hillyard is complete without writing about his wife. Her influence touches every page.

At the most basic level it was Blanche's money, or her father's, that allowed George Hillyard to lead such a privileged lifestyle. Equally, on a sporting level, Blanche was already the Wimbledon Champion when they married. Hillyard was a decent player, but not then of the first rank. The world of tennis at that time belonged much more to his new wife although it was one he embraced with a will. Hillyard was a sportsman and competitor, and a successful one to boot. In those early days, he would have been entering tournaments and often losing early whilst Blanche reached finals and took prizes. Hillyard was a proud man, and nothing would have spurred him on quite as much as the desire to emulate the achievements of his new wife. This said, as time passed and his own tennis improved, so their marriage evolved and he became more sanguine about her status.

Victorian attitudes to women playing sport were very different from those of today. Sport was often referred to as 'weakening,' and women were discouraged from putting in any kind of extreme effort in case it made them ill. Any more than a walk to reach the ball, or at most a gentle amble, was considered unladylike. The position of women in society was much more circumscribed. There were boys' public schools followed by gentlemen's clubs for men to escape to, but most middle class girls were taught at home and, as adults, existed more in the drawing-room than the world outside. Playing or watching sport allowed young women to meet young men in a relaxed way, and there were few other opportunities in society for this to happen - which is presumably one of the reasons that the playing of sport by women was looked upon so negatively by the patriarchal elements in society. But times were changing, at least a little, and despite some opposition it began to be accepted that sport was actually a healthy and positive thing for women to be doing, subtly encouraging qualities of independence and strength of character.

George Hillyard would have been aware of both views, and influenced by each. He was very much a product of the 'Man's world' of public school, Royal Navy, male amateur sport, and gentleman's clubs. I imagine that at first he found some contradictions in finding his new bride so feted and admired in her role as a sporting star. As their relationship strengthened, it's clear he came to take genuine pride in her record of achievement.

In his book, he was forced to write a chapter on ladies tennis as Blanche refused. This left him the task of running through the list of champions, and giving each a pen portrait. He is complimentary about the abilities of Lottie Dod, but makes a strong case that his wife was catching up with her by the time Dod retired.

He writes: *In 1893, on the only two occasions they met, there was little to choose between them, from a match-winning point of view. At the Northern Championships Mrs Hillyard was 5-4, 40-15, in the final set, and again with match point at advantage. Whilst a week or so later, at Wimbledon, they were a set all with Miss Dod winning the final set 6-4.*

Blanche serving, with a very basic overarm action. Before 1910 the majority of lady players served underarm, including Wimbledon champions Maud Watson and Lottie Dod. When I was a child much of my earliest tennis was with an elderly neighbour, Miss Roud, who used to drive me out to her tennis club when there was no-one else for her to play. She had a wicked underarm sidespin serve that I could rarely return, and she wouldn't let me reciprocate ('you MUST serve overarm or you'll never learn to serve properly!') So Miss Roud would serve underarm and I'd double fault and she'd mop me up, even in her sixties. Once I suggested she serve overarm. 'In my day all ladies served underarm,' she insisted. Considering she might have started playing tennis in the late 1910s there was probably some truth in this

Lottie Dod was a sporting phenomenon of her time. Blanche, in the year of her marriage, lost her first Wimbledon title to Dod, and then had to face defeat against her in four more finals. On every occasion that Dod won Wimbledon, it was Blanche she beat in the final. The only year Blanche became champion was when Dod failed to enter. This would have been disheartening but Blanche was never one to give up. Her determination and willingness to fight on to the last gasp were always her greatest strengths. By 1893 the gap does seem to have been closing, with Blanche only losing narrowly in two long matches, having held three match points in one of these.

Following 1893 Dod retired and the opportunity for Blanche to beat her was forever lost. It's somehow touching that 30 years later George Hillyard is still fighting his wife's corner.

Hillyard admits that Dod was the better player in terms of technique and variety of shot. But, he says: *In*

Mrs Hillyard she was up against a player who could cover as much court as Mlle Lenglen, who was a match player of the highest order, and who never knew when she was beaten or what it was to be tired; also, and above all, she was possessed of a forehand drive unique in the history of ladies play … Those who did not encounter Mrs Hillyard at her very best (in the years '93 to '97, after which her powers began to wane) can have no conception of the pace that this drive came off the ground.

Elsewhere Hillyard also tells a story of his friend and Wimbledon Champion, Harold Mahoney, who had a strong game with a relatively weak forehand, watching Blanche's stroke in envious despair and wishing he could hit with confidence at such a pace. I came across a recent description which spoke of her hitting topspin on the forehand side, but from reading contemporary accounts my impression is more of a very fast and flat stroke with a full follow-through (which is said to have sometimes left bruises on her back as the racquet completed its swing).

Blanche, Brookes, and beagle at Thorpe Satchville. Blanche and Norman Brookes were regular mixed doubles partners when he was in England.

Blanche was a less technically orthodox player than her husband. Looking at pictures and articles of the time, it seems she played much of her game using her forehand grip, which contributed to making her volley weak, and her backhand quite defensive, and mostly played with slice. The serve was overarm but hit quite square to the net without a classic service grip – it would have been accurate but lacking in variation.

But despite her technical limitations, if a player is a champion of their time, whatever the era, then they have achieved all that any player can. In summary, Blanche's strengths were her speed of foot, allied to a 'weapon' forehand, and a love for the game. Even more important than any of these Blanche was a superb competitor. She relished a battle, despite the fact that the battle would have been waged wearing clothing

These photos may be faded having lain unseen inside the Hillyard's album for more than a hundred years, but I think they are superb!

Here is Blanche getting ready to strike a backhand. Her racquet-face is closed and a lifted backhand looks likely – not what I expected from contemporary descriptions of her game where a slice backhand seemed more generally played.

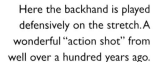

Here the backhand is played defensively on the stretch. A wonderful "action shot" from well over a hundred years ago.

completely inappropriate for any athletic encounter. When tennis began there was no specific tennis wear, and lady competitors wore what they wore in general – a long dress that reached down to, and covered, the ankles, petticoats and a corset, a buttoned-down shirt with a high collar, long sleeves and cuffs that reached to the wrists, a tie, boots, and a hat. The primary goal was to cover any glimpse of flesh, below the upper part of the neck. The only exception to this rule was that the hands were left uncovered, although not by Blanche who mostly wore thin calf-skin gloves to give a better grip on the racquet.

As tennis developed, the wearing of white became the norm, partly because it was said to be the best colour to hide ladies perspiration. The sheer volume of women's clothing became a little less, but the length

To the left is Blanche, around 1900, in tennis gear. Bar her face, not an inch of flesh is showing. To the right, Blanche and her beagles, relaxing at Thorpe Satchville.

remained much the same right up to the first war, particularly for women, like Blanche, of the Victorian generation. May Sutton, the visiting American champion, did attempt, in 1905, to wear a blouse that left her forearms partially uncovered, and a skirt that allowed her ankles and an inch or two of leg to be visible. She can be seen wearing such an outfit, alone amongst the other women, in one of the group photos at Thorpe Satchville, although at Wimbledon she was ordered to have the skirt lengthened to hide her ankles before she was allowed onto court.

It was noted that running back to hit the smash ladies would sometimes trip over the trailing hem of their skirt – no wonder men were expected to cover the lob at mixed doubles!

In 1890 Herbert W. Wilberforce wrote a book titled '*Lawn Tennis: with a chapter for Ladies.*' The chapter for ladies was written by Blanche Hillyard. It was quite short, but Blanche's name would have given the book a certain cachet, particularly amongst the hoped-for lady readers. Wilberforce had won the Wimbledon doubles in 1887 and his book proved popular, enjoying many reprints up to 1908.

Within the book, Wilberforce describes mixed doubles play (or 'mixed pairs' as it was then called), thus: *no doubt very pleasant and charming from a social point of view, but looking at the game scientifically not of much value… A four in which two good players are linked to two bad ones is at best a poor performance… As mere exercise most men will find playing with a feeble partner against a strong pair perfectly satisfying… It is better to take the service, the lady's return of a good service being generally not quite what it should be… any stroke he sends to the lady on the other side he is disappointed if he does not win… should ask the lady to take the right-hand court ; she is probably not very strong on the backhand, The drawback is that one is generally one stroke behind… in the rare cases where one's partner can volley, of course her best place will be at the net, and only two yards off. If she cannot volley, the extreme corner of the court will be the best place for her… When the lady is serving to the man, unless she has an unusually good service, her partner should stand near the middle of the base line, say from a yard to two yards from it… if the lady is returning the service, her partner should be at the back of the court; if he is returning it, she should be at the extreme corner: and this even if she is a good player, because, unless her partner is extraordinarily bad, he is bound to be better than she is and therefore ought to have the large majority of the strokes…. Many ladies will be entirely nonplussed by a high underhand twisted service, and few can take them with much effect… Sometimes, when the man is having a sort of duel with the lady, he will notice the other man edging nearer and nearer, preparing to cut in to his partner's relief; he may then suddenly place the ball across the man or down his line as the case may be, and take him completely by surprise.*

What a great picture! It is amongst those given to Michael Charles, but also features in Hillyard's book. Hillyard stands next to his favourite Wimbledon partner, Clem Cazalet. Blanche is flanked by May Sutton and Miss Wilson to the left and the Dohertys to the right. Marjorie sits in front of Laurie.

Of course, attitudes were very different then, and I'm sure there was many a time that ladies would have had to hold their tongues on the tennis court. But even for his time, one has to imagine that Wilberforce might have been considered particularly insufferable. It seems unlikely that the ladies were queuing up to partner him! And so why did Blanche contribute the chapter? Was she herself of a similar opinion to Wilberforce?

Well, no she wasn't. But Wilberforce was her husband's friend and therefore her own friend as well. His views on mixed doubles might have been demeaning, but he himself would not have considered them as such and they were widely held.

Anyway, Blanche wrote the chapter. At the request of Wilberforce, she was asked to aim it at lady beginners - perhaps he felt that all women players were simply beginners when compared to men.

Blanche gave some simple tips, and then spoke about dress in a way which was quite revolutionary for 1890: *Nothing is more uncomfortable than a heavy narrow skirt ; and I find that one made of the lightest possible material, not less than 2.5 yards in width, gives the greatest freedom in getting about the court. I assume that the usual shoes with India rubber soles will be worn, as it would, of course, be impossible to play in ordinary walking boots. The hat, too, should be one which, while shading your face, will not be inconveniently large.*

She concludes with a possible dig at Wilberforce: *In conclusion, there can be no doubt that lawn tennis is a most healthy and invigorating exercise for ladies, and is at present the one game in which a girl can to some extent hold her own with men; and I am sure, if only more ladies would take it up and play regularly, they would be far more healthy and strong.*

Like her husband, Blanche enjoyed travelling to Europe and playing on 'sand' courts. Playing abroad extended both the social and the tennis seasons, and was therefore an experience to be warmly welcomed. In 1903, at a time when she had already won her six Wimbledon titles, Wallis Myers wrote an appreciation of Blanche:

Let me just recall here a few facts about this celebrated lady's lawn tennis career, which must astonish all who remember her in the front rank twenty years ago.

Nothing more wonderful has ever been done by any lady at the premier meeting. Except on five occasions when she did not compete, from 1885, when she first won the 'All-Comers' at Wimbledon, down to 1901, Mrs. Hillyard has either been the 'runner-up' or the holder of the championship. Another record, perhaps even more striking, is her number of victories in first-class Open singles, which amount to fifty-eight. On six occasions she has won the Championship of England, on ten occasions the South of England Championship, three times the Northern Championship, and three times the Irish Championship. Mrs. Hillyard has not been attracted much to the covered courts, but on the only occasion she competed for the Ladies' Championship it fell to her racket.

In Doubles her successes have been quite as numerous. I need, perhaps, only instance here her two successes in this department with Ernest Renshaw and Wilfred Baddeley respectively ; her two victories at Dublin with G. W. Hillyard and G. Greville respectively; and the Covered Court Mixed Championship with her husband on the only occasion she entered the lists. Mrs. Hillyard has also done another thing that no other lady has ever done, nor, it is pretty safe to say, will ever do— she has won the Ladies' Doubles Championship (four times with Miss Steedman), five years in succession.

Her travels over the border and abroad have been productive of many successes. She has been Champion of Wales, Champion of Germany twice, of the South of France and of Monte Carlo. Never has such a zealous, conscientious and self-possessed lady appeared on any court; and it is only stating a bare fact to say that her experience of the game and its leading exponents, stretching as it does over at least two generations, is unique. The Hillyards have, as I have previously said, a fine court of their own in Leicestershire, and here the ex-champion for the most part keeps 'her hand in.' On horseback Mrs. Hillyard is as capable as with the racket; during the winter months she is a keen and expert rider with the hounds; and in other sports, like her husband, she excels.

In the context of tennis history, Blanche has a remarkable place. Of course, in her day the champion from the previous year did not have to 'play through' to reach the final – instead she stood out and had just one match against the winner of the 'all-comers' event. But, in fact, because Blanche twice stopped playing tennis to have children, of her six Wimbledon titles only one, the last in 1900, was won as the reigning champion. In all of her five previous Wimbledon wins she came through the entire draw, just as today. Certainly the number of competitors was less than now, but the draws were not seeded which increased the likelihood of coming up against the best players in the early rounds.

Left, Blanche and Jack, around 1895.

Left: Blanche with a dog that may or may not be a beagle, about the same time

Blanche was also the first mother to win Wimbledon, in 1894, three years after giving birth to Jack. This is a feat achieved, rather surprisingly, by only three other players in history – Evonne Goolagong Cawley being the most recent. Blanche also won the title another three times after the birth of her second child, Marjorie, in 1896.

The years of her six Wimbledon wins were 1885, 1889, 1894, 1897, 1899, and 1900. The 15 year gap between first and last championship wins remains a record to this day, as are her 13 appearance in a Wimbledon singles final (although this would have been facilitated by the champion 'standing out'). She lost in the final for the last time at the age of 37. Her ultimate win at the age of 36 makes her the oldest champion bar Charlotte Cooper Stery who was 37 when she won in 1908. (Stery actually beat Blanche in 1901 and was a regular at the Thorpe Satchville tennis parties with her husband, Alfred).

Miss Toupie Lowther, writing in the Badminton magazine in 1903 said: *Everyone must have a great admiration for Mrs Hillyard. She has played and won more matches than any other lady player. To assure oneself of this fact, one has only to pay her a visit at her home in Leicestershire, where the number of trophies one sees in the shape of cups is almost incredible. She is a most determined player, and never loses heart, but plays on with the same indomitable pluck and energy to the last stroke.*

In his book, Hillyard includes a story by Miss Lowther of a match against his wife. Miss Lowther was due to play Blanche in the handicap event at Homburg. The thought of playing the Wimbledon champion, or as she says: '*Mrs Hillyard, the innumerable times Champion!*' – left her in a state of nervous panic. She continues: *So much so that when I walked on to the court and began the match, the balls seemed to have shrunk to the size of marbles, the net to have stretched in height like Alice in Wonderland, and my accuracy departed to such an extent that I wondered whether I had been born cross-eyed.*

Miss Lowther had not previously met the Champion; rather she had worshipped her from afar. Blanche was giving away odds of 30-0 in one game, then 15-0 the next, but still won the first set easily, 6-1. She was playing perfectly and placing the ball wherever she wanted: *until panting and distressed, in body and mind, discouraged and despairing, I swore to myself that never would I play in a tournament again.*

The two players went to change ends, and Blanche stopped Miss Lowther and began shouting at her. '*Why on Earth don't you try? Of course I can't give you these odds, if only you will play up. It's perfectly sickening playing someone who doesn't try. Don't be such a damned fool! Stick to it and you'll win!'*

Miss Lowther concludes: *The effect of this encouragement by a perfect stranger, and still more the somewhat dramatic and peculiar method of giving it, was magical. I felt so 'bucked' as the schoolboys say, that my nervousness left me entirely, and I won the match!*

A good story – although one wonders whether, in the event, Mrs Hillyard was left wishing she had kept her thoughts to herself!

After this match Toupie Lowther became a close friend of the Hillyards, and she was mentioned in his book as one of the great players of the day, although of uneven temperament. Wallis Myers wrote of her, with words that may have had a subtle hidden meaning: *If Miss Toupee Lowther had not devoted most of her leisure to sport—sport of a strenuous, masculine type—one could almost picture her leading a public movement in favour of 'Woman's Rights.' For she is essentially a lady of strong personality, destined to command, and her knowledge of men and women is so wide, her disregard of petty restrictions so pronounced, that apparently nothing would stop her if she once made up her mind publicly to support a policy of emancipation.* He went on to list her accomplishments, not just in tennis, but also as a brilliant fencer, a driver, a musician, and *a passionate convert to the mysteries of Ju-jitsu.*

To continue to stray temporarily from the subject of Blanche, although hopefully down an interesting fork, in 1917 Toupie Lowther became famous for raising money for an all-women ambulance service of 25 drivers and 20 ambulances which transported thousands of injured soldiers away from the front, travelling on bombed-out roads and facing frequent shelling. She now features in numerous books, and is cited as a notable 20th century lesbian, and an example of female masculinity. Whether Toupie would have been happy with these descriptions is not known. Certainly there is a story, which may be apocryphal, that she was arrested for masquerading as a man while crossing the Franco-Italian border wearing trousers. On her return she wore a skirt to avoid controversy, and was then arrested for masquerading as a woman. On arriving at the front with her 20 ambulances, the French refused to allow access to the lines on the grounds that women should not put themselves deliberately in harm's way. She met with a large group of French Officers, the leader of whom said: 'Am I to send you to possible death?' To which Toupie replied: *'I am of the opinion that a few women less in the world is of no importance.'* She was subsequently allowed to take the ambulances to the front, where her bravery, and that of her female drivers, saved lives until the end of the war.

Alfred Stery related an affectionate reminiscence of Blanche: *I first had the pleasure of meeting Mrs Hillyard at the Hamburg tournament in 1897. She was always an untiring enthusiast for the game and even when her matches for the day were over would be anxious to get up a four with anyone who could play regardless of their capabilities. I was fortunate to be asked to play with her in these games which were most enjoyable. We were staying at the same hotel and one day whilst travelling to the ground she asked me if I would like to play in the handicap mixed at Eastbourne. She was the Wimbledon Lady Champion and her invitation was so surprising I nearly fell off the tram seat from shock. I murmured that I had not anticipated going to Eastbourne but I should certainly do so now.*

With little experience of tournaments I entered for the three handicap events and arrived at Eastbourne on Monday to find that handicaps didn't commence until later in the week. Finally on Wednesday I was called onto Number One court to play the first round of the mixed. I went on court praying for an earthquake and in the first set was so horribly nervous that when

I did hit the ball over the net it surprised everyone, though I was receiving the most wonderful encouragement from my sporting partner. Notwithstanding my feeble efforts, Mrs Hillyard played as if she was contesting the final at Wimbledon, and thanks to her fine play we survived the first round.

Still in the event on finals day, Stery had to wait for Mrs Hillyard to play the final of the ladies singles, where she lost surprisingly to Miss Cooper. Stery continues: *Hardly was the match over when she said: 'Let us get on with the handicap mixed.'* To cut a long story short, we won the event and, as she told a friend afterwards, *'If someone had told me the only event I should win at Eastbourne was the handicap mixed I shouldn't have believed them.'*

Possibly Stery's most memorable image is that of Mrs Hillyard, Wimbledon champion, searching for a scratch foursome to have a friendly doubles match at the end of a busy day's play in a tournament. Not easy to imagine the top stars of today doing this!

Blanche's love for tennis meant that she continued to enter tournaments long after her powers were on the wane. She never worried about defending her status – she simply enjoyed playing tennis for as long as she could, and in as many events as possible. Her record of tournament wins is unparalleled, at singles, doubles, and mixed (as well in handicaps!) An incomplete list of singles championships includes, the Irish, Welsh, North of England, London, Cheltenham, Ashby, Middlesex, Buxton, Nottingham, Exmouth, British covered courts, Leicester, German, South of France, Cannes and Monte Carlo. A particular favourite was the South of England Championships at Eastbourne where she won the singles title on 11 occasions.

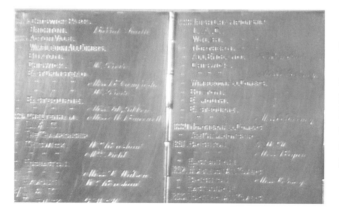

Well, here's something you don't see every day!!! This is a solid silver memorial to every tennis tournament that Blanche Hillyard ever won. It was presented to her by an unknown (to me) admirer It was handed down to Jack Hillyard, Blanche's son and is now in the possession of his step-daughter Ada Dawnay. It is a wonderful, unique and extremely generous memento.

The dates stretch from Blanche's first to her last tournament victory covering 10 sides of small lettering on silver. So many victories!!! And what a wonderful present.

I have recently been told that Blanche could be quite critical of her partner at mixed, or at least when this partner was her husband. Evidently the sound of Blanche shouting loudly in despair when George missed a shot was quite a common occurrence in tournament play at that time. Is this likely? And was it ever thus, or a habit that crept upon them as the years passed? I suppose it's something we'll never know for sure but, to me, it does ring strangely true.

In photographs Blanche is notably grim, although this didn't necessarily reflect her general temperament. She was an excellent host and a valued friend. Her wit was admittedly acerbic, but she did possess a keen sense of humour. She was a loving mother – in fact almost the only thing that stopped her playing tennis tournaments was the birth of her children!

Blanche Hillyard was athletic, able, competitive and independent. She was a strong woman beyond the confines of the home, and despite the status and energy of her husband she was never in his shadow. She was a substantial personality in her own right who achieved in terms of results and longevity a remarkable tennis record that may never be equalled.

16

PULBOROUGH, AND THE WEST SUSSEX GOLF CLUB

*I*n 1925, a year after his book was published and at the age of 61, George Hillyard resigned from his position as Secretary of the All England Club, leaving to his successor the privilege of celebrating the 50th anniversary of the Wimbledon Championships.

In the same year he put his Leicestershire house on the market. Thorpe Satchville had been his home for 30 years – a centre not just for his family, but also for his social and sporting life. He speaks sadly of sifting through his old papers and finding notes of matches played on his courts: *Too many ghosts would crowd in and obtrude. Too many good men and true, whose deeds were recorded, had joined the majority. Ernest and Willie Renshaw, Mahoney, the two Dohertys, W. V. Eaves, Lionel Enscombe, Wilding, R. B. Powell, Kenneth Powell (the last three killed in the war) – all have gone; and others. No, old diaries are not perused altogether with impunity or unmixed feelings.*

These were all athletic, sporting men, many of whom never reached fifty, and often not even forty. Lives were shorter then, and he clearly feels the loss of his friends.

Leaving Thorpe Satchville must have been hard, of course, but it was time to move on. Sir George Earle came to inspect the property. He expressed an interest, and at the same time spoke glowingly about his own home at Bramfold in Pulborough. Hillyard wondered if something might be done by way of an exchange and travelled down to Sussex to have a look. He liked what he saw, and the pair swapped houses.

Whether there was an additional payment, and on which side, isn't known. But it's quite a typical spur-of-the-moment Hillyard action and, in fact, the two houses are remarkably similar. Neither was old at the time. Both are large properties on two storeys with rooms enough for crowded house-parties, set in large grounds of several acres. Each is in a very rural area, well away from city life.

The only photograph I have of Hillyard at Bramfold. He would have been well over 60 and is pictured by the house on what was the en-tout-cas hard court.

He went to Sussex to retire, or this is what I assumed when I first began my researches. The time had evidently come to relax and rest, and reflect on a life well-spent. And Hillyard *did* retire, in the sense that he was no longer Secretary of the All England Club. He maintained, however, a number of very close and important links with the Wimbledon tournament. He became Director of the Championships from 1926 to 1928, and then a member of the Tournament Executive from 1929 all the way through to 1939. He also continued umpiring on Centre Court in the final of the ladies singles.

So his duties were now directed much more towards the championships themselves, rather than the general year-round running of the club. With the ending of his day-to-day responsibilities, he looked around for new challenges, and found them in the game of golf.

On one side his new house faced out onto a large area of sandy ground and heather, totally surrounded by marsh stretching away into the distance. Today the view at ground level is largely obscured by trees, but in Hillyard's time it was more open. From the upstairs windows, even now, the view is impressive, and then it would surely have been one of the great pleasures of the property. It wasn't long before he eyed the wide vista of virgin land, and imagined it being put to more practical use.

Unsurprisingly, though, the first thing he did after his move was to construct two tennis courts, one grass and one shale, with the hard court certainly built by En-tout-cas, and possibly the grass as well. The tennis courts, still visible, are placed on the panoramic side of the house, the shale court to the left and the grass court to the right. Each has handsome, now neglected, steps leading down to it, and remnants of the

The site of the En-tout-cas shale court at Bramfold – Hillyard's house in Pulborough

On the right are the old steps leading down to the court. But no court remains – just a grassed over space

hedges and fencing which would have separated and sheltered the courts from the rest of the grounds. Sadly neither is now in use; both are given over to lawn with the shale court turfed over by a more recent owner. When the light falls in a certain way then the ghostly traces of tennis lines can faintly be seen on the space which the grass court previously inhabited. But that is all that remains of Hillyard's original courts.

Bramfold House – the outline of the old grass court is visible to the right of the swimming pool
The old shale court is not shown on the aerial view and is further along on the right

Below Andrew Moffat, current owner of Bramfold House stands on the old grass court. Behind is the house

A more permanent monument to his efforts than his two abandoned tennis courts stands on the land which provided such a perfect view from those upper windows; land which is now home to the West Sussex Golf Club.

Hillyard's sporting career had always been varied – as Herbert Chipp wrote in his book 'Lawn Tennis Recollections': *Of all the lawn tennis players of the present day, G W Hillyard undoubtedly ranks as the best all-round athlete. He had always been a keen golfer – the nine hole golf course in his home at Thorpe Satchville was of high quality and often-used, and Hillyard was of a standard to more than match his golf course.*

In his early years cricket had been his passion, then tennis took centre stage after his marriage to Blanche. In Thorpe Satchville he had also been able to play a short round of golf between sets of tennis. Now situated in Pulborough, tennis courts constructed, he decided he would once again like a convenient golf course just a short stroll from his back gate.

The best sight lines from Hillyard's bedroom window (but not his bathroom window, as legend suggested, from which the view was not good at all) were to the eventual 3rd Green and 7th Fairway.
Here is a view from the 7th tee – natural heather showing in abundance. This, and the next 3 excellent photographs of West Sussex Golf Club, were taken by West Sussex member, Daisy Kane.

The official history of West Sussex Golf Club takes up the tale: *It was Commander George Hillyard who conceived the idea of a golf club on sandy farmland at Wiggonholt near Pulborough. His house overlooked an area of heather and marsh which he thought would make an idyllic setting for a natural course. How right he was! … It was an immediate success, as illustrated in this extract from The Morning Post dated Thursday 4th September 1930:- 'The course is laid out over a heather moor, rising suddenly and surprisingly out of meadow and marshland that is characteristic of Sussex….It is absolutely ideal golfing country … Every type of hole and shot in the game is there.'*

Local legend has it that Hillyard was standing at his bathroom window, engaged in a morning shave, when the idea suddenly struck him that the land below might make an ideal golf course. This is a good story, but unlikely. More probably, he would have known instinctively from the first that the neighbouring grounds were a suitable site for a golf course – the problem would have been finding a practical way to bring his idea to fruition.

Perhaps a number of other people might have seen the possibilities on offer, but most would simply have left it at that. Maybe a casual 'Do you know what would be a good idea?', and then let the matter drop so that twenty or thirty years later the land in question would be covered in concrete. But Hillyard was always made of sterner stuff. Nothing if not resourceful, he was the ideal man for the job. His experience with the epic project at Church Road would have been a perfect preparation for such a sizeable venture as a golf course. He was also a great persuader and a man with good connections. The most difficult task would be raising the cash.

Thanks to information provided by West Sussex Golf Club, I can quote from an undated letter written in 1928 by Hillyard in which he sets about the task. In it he explained his idea for the course, and proposed a system of debentures to raise capital. The letter would have been sent to his neighbours, but clearly he had already spoken to some in person and gained their support.

The view towards the 3ʳᵈ green, from the direction of Bramfold, the house of George Hillyard.

He notes: *I have received already such substantial support as to encourage me to proceed further with the project. Wherefore if it meets your approval will you help to make it a practical possibility by taking up Debentures of one sort or another?*

The letter did the trick, and moved matters forward. The accompanying architect's report was by Cecil Hutchison and Guy Campbell who were well respected golf course architects. It was a single page, and extremely positive. It says: *The ground is entirely suitable for the purpose of constructing an absolutely first class 18 holes inland course. The general contour of ground is excellent with unique natural features … the course would compare favourably with any of the famous inland courses in Britain.* It concludes: *We can see no reason why a course should not be constructed for an approximate sum of £5,000 which would eventually equal such famous courses as Gleneagles, Sunningdale and Walton Heath.*

'Laying it on quite thick,' is a phrase that springs to mind when reading the architect's report, but clearly it worked, although another letter from Hillyard sent on September 1928 sought to chivvy people along. He notes that three more architects have inspected the site of the proposed course and : *All three are equally enthusiastic as to its merits, even going so far as to say that it might be made into the best inland course in England. This is very high praise indeed, and with such extraordinary possibilities it seems a pity if the scheme falls through.*

To progress matters further he called a meeting of interested parties, to be held at his house on Saturday October 13th 1928 at 4.30pm. 136 circulars had been sent with 28 positive responses. As a result, £5000 was promised but this still left the project £8000 short of its target. He remarked: *Matters now are rather at a standstill, and I think that the only thing to be done is to call a meeting of all those who have so kindly and generously taken an interest in the project, discuss it as a whole and see if anything further can be suggested towards its accomplishment.*

The meeting was productive. Amongst the interested neighbouring landowners were two married couples, the Ravenscrofts and the Hendersons - relative newcomers to Sussex, who generously offered to buy the entire estate of Hurston Warren themselves. They would then lease back to the club whatever land it needed for the course. Later on they also paid for the new clubhouse, having it built as a large country house in case the golf club should fail and they would have to sell. It was over a game of bridge that the Ravenscrofts and the Hendersons supposedly made the decision. With the cost of the land put at £3,000 this would have been the decisive news which turned Hillyard's golf course from dream to reality.

The West Sussex clubhouse was built as a large country house in case the golf club should fail and the investors would have something to sell. This photo is so idyllic that it almost looks like a painting, but it's not – this is how the clubhouse really looks!

The main facilitators for the course now became Hillyard, Colonel Ravenscroft and Philip Henderson. They were part of a small Council of Officers who moved the project forward at an incredibly fast pace that would be impossible today. During March 1929 the first officers of the club were appointed. Ravenscroft was to be Club Captain and Henderson Vice-Captain. Hillyard was given responsibility for 'wellbeing of course, greens, fairways and links,' – effectively Chairman of Greens.

There is just one foolscap sized plan in the club archives which shows the outline of the original course designed by Links and Courses Ltd, the architectural firm of 'The Three Majors' - Hutchison, Campbell and Hotchkin. Although undated and unsigned, it bears many handwritten notes and amendments in Hillyard's unmistakeable hand, showing clearly how much interest he had in the design and construction.

Hole 18 at West Sussex with a particularly fine view of the clubhouse and to the Downs beyond. Isn't it beautiful?
If I didn't love tennis so much I might take up golf!

The job of building the course was given to En-tout-cas. The decision to offer them the contract was at the recommendation of Hillyard, ratified by the council.

George Hillyard and En-tout-cas had a close relationship from the first day he met Claude Brown and discussed the use of crushed bricks to produce a tennis court. The surface was excellent for the time, but would have needed promotion, and this is something Hillyard was in a perfect position to do, both in his role as Secretary of the All England Club, and as a highly-respected player with excellent contacts throughout the tennis world. Then in the war it was Hillyard who came to the company's rescue by helping with Government contracts. Later, when Wimbledon was moved to Church Road, he managed to funnel the work for the nine new hard courts to En-tout-cas, giving them a marketing coup which would have been a gold-plated recommendation for future work and finance.

In today's equivalent terms, at its peak En-tout-cas was a multi-million pound business. Hillyard himself seems to have had little money when he married Blanche in 1887. Blanche was an heiress and presumably funded the purchase of Thorpe Satchville and much of their ensuing relaxed lifestyle. Later Blanche bred beagles, and Hillyard was Wimbledon Club Secretary. The couple also took to renting their Leicestershire home to rich Americans during the hunting season. None of this would have generated enough income to cover their yearly expenses. In the course of my researches I began to wonder whether it might be possible that Hillyard received some reward from the company for his quiet support, although it seemed to be something not easily provable either way.

The answer was found in the minutes kindly provided by West Sussex golf club of the same council meeting in which Hillyard recommended En-tout-cas as builders. It states that in accordance with their Articles of Association *Commander Hillyard formally disclosed to the Council that he was a Director of the En-tout-cas company.*

In 1903 Hillyard beat Harold Hilton in Cannes at golf – as Hilton was twice British Open champion in 1892 and 1897 this was a remarkable sporting achievement.
These photos are from Hillyard's album and are most likely taken in Cannes.

This seems to indicate that Hillyard did indeed receive income from En-tout-cas. And whatever the date he became Company Director, this wouldn't have precluded an earlier less formal arrangement to provide financial advantage in return for promoting the company's interests. Whatever the case, it should be stressed that En-tout-cas had a genuine reputation for providing work of a high standard. At West Sussex Golf Club, Mr Carr was foreman of the construction team. His contribution was so satisfactory to Hillyard and the Club Council that they presented him with a £20 gratuity and an inscribed leather wallet when he handed over the course as completed and sown on August 8th 1930.

Once the course was in play Hillyard was given total responsibility for its management, as well as £500 to be spent on development 'as he sees fit.' By January 1931 he submitted his report on all this work, clearly helped by the experience gained both in his time at Wimbledon, and in the projects over the years at home. In all he constructed 15 new tees, reshaped and deepened bunkers on 13 holes, introduced new bunkers on three holes, as well as removing others. Finally the course was ready for its official opening in April 1931.

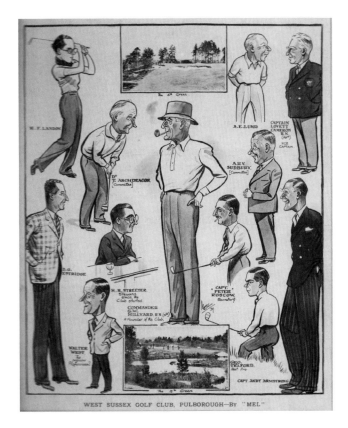

WEST SUSSEX GOLF CLUB, PULBOROUGH—BY "MEL"

Two of the pictures of Hillyard which still hang in the excellent West Sussex clubhouse.
Above the Commander in his uniform.
To the left, Hillyard stands centre-stage, hands on hips.

Initially, as might be expected, there were a few teething troubles on the course, with problems of drainage, turf and general playability. But money for improvements was suddenly short, due to the Wall Street Crash of 1929 and the ensuing financial depression which reached across the Atlantic. Eventually, in October 1932, a further sum of £700 was made available to allow Hillyard to bring the course up to the highest quality. Part of this grant was used to change the 6th and 10th holes, relocate the tees on the 11th and to change the 13th hole. The 15th green was also rebuilt and re-laid. In the absence of any course architects, George Hillyard directed the work himself.

The list of early Club Captains makes interesting reading. The idea that the Club Captain is next to God in a Golf Club (and even then over matters of dress you ask the Captain first) makes this an important social record. In 1930 the first was Colonel Ravenscroft. Next in 1931 was Philip Henderson. Then in 1932 it was the turn of Cmdr G. H. Hillyard. Clearly money came before invention, and why not!

George Hillyard's portrait, painted by Charles Ambrose, now hangs in the West Sussex lounge. His notable contribution to the club is acknowledged by the Hillyard Trophy which is still competed for.

The Times, on May 20 1949, wrote: *On June 11 there will take place on the course of the West Sussex Club at Pulborough, the first open competition for the George Hillyard Memorial Cup. The late G.W. Hillyard was the discoverer*

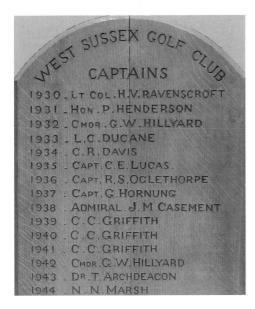

WEST SUSSEX GOLF CLUB
CAPTAINS
1930 - Lt Col. H.V. RAVENSCROFT
1931 - Hon. P. HENDERSON
1932 - Cmdr. G.W. HILLYARD
1933 - L.C. DUCANE
1934 - C.R. DAVIS
1935 - Capt. C.E. LUCAS.
1936 - Capt. R.S. OGLETHORPE
1937 - Capt. G. HORNUNG
1938 - ADMIRAL J.M. CASEMENT
1939 - C.C. GRIFFITH
1940 - C.C. GRIFFITH
1941 - C.C. GRIFFITH
1942 - Cmdr. G.W. HILLYARD
1943 - Dr. T. ARCHDEACON
1944 - N.N. MARSH

To the left is the Captain's Board. Hillyard's name appears in 1932 and 1942. To the right is the superb portrait by Charles Ambrose which hangs in the West Sussex clubhouse. In total there are 3 pictures in appreciation of Hillyard at West Sussex – a credit to him, and the club

of this, one of the best and sandiest of inland courses: he devoted treasures of care and affection to it as long as he lived and this challenge cup has been given in his memory. The competition is open to all amateurs having handicaps of 4 or less, and the cup will be held for a year by the player having the best scratch score over 36 holes. The competition and the course alike deserve a strong field.

In Mark Rowlinson's book 'The World Atlas of Golf – the greatest courses and how they are played,' he says: *You could hardly describe Pulborough as being a London suburb for it is deep in the Sussex countryside, but here is to be found the very last and farthest outcrop of 'Surrey' heathland in England. It is the home of the West Sussex Golf Club.*

For those who love their golf to be conducted in absolute peace and quiet and in over-rewardingly challenging terrain, a debt of gratitude is owed to the wandering eye of Commander George Hillyard. These were precisely the qualities that turned a routine early morning shave into something far more significant.

From the bathroom window of his rather grand home Commander Hillyard recognized that the landscape before him was the natural setting for a golf course. Tennis was Hillyard's game — he was a Wimbledon doubles finalist in 1891 and secretary of the All England Lawn Tennis & Croquet Club (1907-21) — but he also clearly had a more than capable eye for golfing terrain.

Soon after spotting the potential of this tract of sandy heathland, it was bought and leased to West Sussex. The course was designed by Major C K Hutchinson who with James Braid had been responsible for Gleneagles, and with Guy Campbell for Prince's GC at Sandwich. Stafford Vere Hopkin was also involved. Between them they created a course that has more than maintained its youth, and to this day provides glorious golf in the most tranquil of locations.

It finishes with: Renovation has not been, and still is not, required, and it might be suspected that Commander Hillyard could have predicted as much when he gazed from his bathroom window all those years ago. He was a man of vision and he made golf in Southern England all the richer for it.

On a couple of points the book is slightly wrong – the dates of Hillyard's time as Wimbledon Secretary, and the idea that no renovation of the course was required – as we've seen there were some changes, and it was Hillyard who supervised them. But overall it is a fair tribute to what is still acknowledged as one of the outstanding inland courses in Britain. So much so that in 2011 West Sussex Golf Club was rated as the best golf course in Sussex and the 76th best golf course in the world!

Hillyard, on the 11th tee, at WSGC.

Above is a picture from 1933 showing the various spaced oak trees and the open farm field along the right side of the 10th hole.

The spot where the photo of Hillyard's drive was taken, and the direction of the take, is marked.

John Kilshaw from West Sussex notes: *Hillyard's fine balanced and full finish and the "splayed foot" action so common in the hickory shaft days.* The companion may have been Charles Ambrose who was a contemporary writer, illustrator, good golfer and friend.

Once constructed, the West Sussex Golf Club became Hillyard's second home, possibly in the same way the All England Club fulfilled this role in previous years. He became a regular fixture at the club, lean and patrician, a notable figure whether striding purposefully across the course or holding court in the clubhouse.

Apart from the large painting, there are two other images of Hillyard on show in the clubhouse. One is a rather impressive framed photograph of Commander Hillyard in his naval uniform. In the other he is the central figure in a small group of pencil caricatures of early members of the club. He is surrounded by ten figures in various poses, with views of the course above and below. Hillyard stands centre-frame, wearing a casual white shirt and wide-brimmed hat, a pipe jammed in his mouth releasing a small cloud of smoke, hands on hips, staring off into the distance like a man who owns the place – of all the pictures I think this might have been his favourite!

Bramfold House is now owned by Andrew Moffat, originally purchased by his father in 1968. For a long time, Andrew's family had no idea that the Hillyards once owned their house. Then, around 25 years ago, Andrew's mother was walking along the lane close to her home when a stranger stopped and asked her if she lived at Bramfold. The questioner had once been a servant of the Hillyards, and the two fell into conversation.

Gone away, but not forgotten. Here is a page from the register of members at the Leicestershire Lawn Tennis Club long after the Hillyards had moved to Sussex. They remained honorary members of the club and their names are noted at the foot of the page

Miss C. M. Hunt	22, Victoria Park Rd.
Mrs. F. H. V. Hunter	Southlea, Elms Rd.
Mrs. Hurst	St. Margaret's Vicarage
Miss E. Hutchinson	Fothoron Lodge, Manor Rd.
Mrs. G. J. Harvey	26, Westminster Rd.
Miss J. Hame	Glenroy. East Avenue
Commander G. W. Hillyard	Pulborough, Sussex.
Mrs. G. W. Hillyard	

Evidently the Hillyards had continued to hold large house parties, just as in Leicestershire. Amongst the guests at Pulborough was reportedly 'the King', most likely George V – Hillyard's boyhood shipmate from HMS Britannia. George V spent some of 1929 recuperating from illness at nearby Bognor (which was renamed Bognor *Regis* in recognition of his stay, and of which he famously said: 'Bugger Bognor!').

Bramfold's royal visitor *might* have been King Edward VIII, the son of George V who later married Wallis Simpson and abdicated after less than a year on the throne. Edward, who was a keen golfer, accepted a proposal from West Sussex that he become president of the club in 1936 – the year of his accession to the throne. Just as at Wimbledon, it was probably Hillyard who asked royalty to become involved with his club, and it's just barely possible that Edward stayed across the road at Bramfold with his father's old friend.

I have been told that in peacetime Hillyard captained the racing yacht *Britannia*, owned in turn by King Edward VII and King George V. It would certainly seem likely that as a close friend and ex-shipmate living not very far away, he would, at least, have been invited on board the yacht by King George to take part in racing during Cowes week and possibly elsewhere. The King was so fond of his yacht that he requested it follow him to the grave. Accordingly, on 10th July 1936, the *Britannia* was towed out to St Catherine's Deep near the Isle of Wight, and sunk.

More conclusive evidence that Hillyard was a regular on the yacht, and possibly captained it, would be the handsome commemorative silver ashtray presented to George Hillyard and constructed from material taken from the *Britannia's* mast. This ashtray was presented to Hillyard after the death of George V, by his son, George VI, and is now in the possession of the Dawnay family. It is inscribed as follows: "MADE FROM THE BOOM OF THE FAMOUS RACING YACHT BRITANNIA, AND GIVEN TO COMMANDER HILLYARD. As a souvenir of his long personal association with her. BY HIS MAJESTY KING GEORGE VI AUGUST 1937."

The silver ashtray presented to Hillyard by King George VI to commemorate his time spent sailing on the Royal Yacht Britannia.

Another reminiscence of the servant concerned Marjorie, the daughter of the house. Marjorie was born in 1896, so would have been in her thirties. She was mentally handicapped, as mentioned earlier, and during house parties would run the length of the long upstairs corridor, banging loudly on the doors of the guests. This story left a strong impression on the current owner. Evidently the house had been plagued by loud bangs and strange occurrences since his childhood, and Andrew remains convinced that the ghost of Marjorie Hillyard still stalks the Bramfold corridors.

I also met Stella Ellis in Pulborough. She was a child newly arrived in the village at the start of the war. She had visited Bramfold a number of times – she would have been nine or ten years old – to ask the groom for advice about her pony. The groom was around 50 years of age and extremely helpful and friendly. She also remembers him talking about his then employer, George Hillyard, and consistently expressing a genuinely warm regard for him. One wonders if the groom had travelled with the family from Thorpe Satchville. Stella went into the house on a number of occasions but remembers little of it. She met Marjorie who was very shy and cut quite an incongruous figure being over six feet tall.

When George Hillyard died, Blanche, with her daughter and a Scottish cook, moved into a cottage in the same lane as Stella. Stella remembers Blanche as quite a frightening elderly lady who possessed an enormous ear trumpet with an amplifier in it. Despite being the daughter of two athletic parents, the only sport that Marjorie could really enjoy was riding, and her mother encouraged her in this. Stella would sometimes ride with her, although Marjorie's mental instability made her a slightly uncomfortable companion for such a young girl.

Stella also related that Marjorie was by then quite a frightened and nervous person who claimed to see ghosts. I mentioned, rather flippantly, Andrew's claim that the house was now haunted by the ghost of Marjorie. Stella told me, quite matter-of-factly, of her own experience on visiting Bramfold for a social occasion many years later after the house had changed hands and was the home of Andrew's mother. Once inside the house, and glancing up the staircase, Stella saw Marjorie Hillyard standing there.

Left are Marjorie and Jack together
Above, Marjorie sits alone
Both photos are taken at Thorpe Satchville

Stella is a very down-to-earth person, and is grateful not to have come across anything supernatural before or since, but believes with complete certainty in the reality of what she saw. Why would Marjorie choose to haunt Bramfold in Sussex rather than Thorpe Satchville in Leicestershire? Maybe because her father died in Bramfold and this made it dear to her? But I don't think I believe in ghosts – although it would seem that both Andrew and Stella do!

17

FINIS

George Hillyard died on 24th March 1943. These were the war years and death was commonplace. In *Lawn Tennis and Badminton* published more than a year later, his obituary was a bare four lines. 'One of the founders of the Association, a leading player of his day, and for many years Secretary of the All England Club.' And that was it.

Blanche Hillyard died three years later, aged 82, on 7th August 1946, in the cottage close by Bramfold. The

Marjorie sits between her mother and father, all clutching beagles, at Thorpe Satchville

cottage is still in existence, and is named 'Greenford', presumably by Blanche who was born in Greenford, Middlesex. Having been born in Greenford, she intended to die there - if it *was* a rather macabre joke, then it seems quite a good one!

By the time of George Hillyard's death most of his tennis contemporaries were long gone. For a man who valued his friendships so highly this must have been particularly sad. Much of his time, in those last years, was spent at the West Sussex Golf Club in an environment removed from tennis. In its third year of existence he had been Club Captain, and he served again in 1942, the year of his death. By then he would have been 79 years of age. Due to the war there may have been a shortage of eligible contenders, but presumably he might also have been given the captaincy as a personal honour. No doubt he would have done his best to fulfil any accompanying duties. I have no details of the manner of his death, but would like to think it occurred whilst hitting a drive on his course (or maybe scratching to get out of a bunker!), or possibly while giving an overlong speech after one of the Captain's dinners.

As we've seen, the Hillyards had two children, Jack and Marjorie. After his father's death Jack would regularly visit his mother and Marjorie at 'Greenford', but he didn't live there. Marjorie spent all her life living with her parents. When her mother died she went to a care home in the West Country, where she stayed until her death.

Hillyard's will was granted probate on 25th May 1943. Blanche Hillyard of Bramfold was 'the lawful widow and relict of the said intestate.' The total estate was worth £926 19s, the net value £710 3s 9d, - not a large amount when set against the sizeable country property that was Bramfold House.

George Hillyard was buried at St Mary's Church, Pulborough, shortly to be joined by Blanche. They lie in the graveyard beneath a single stone with the inscription 'IN MEMORY OF GEORGE WHITESIDE HILLYARD, COMMANDER RN. DIED 24th MARCH 1943 AGED 79. AT THY RIGHT HAND THERE ARE PLEASURES EVER MORE.' And then below this: 'AND HIS WIFE BLANCHE HILLYARD. BORN 3RD NOVEMBER 1863 DIED 7th AUGUST 1946.'

The final resting place of George and Blanche Hillyard in the graveyard at St Mary's Church, Pulborough.

The date on the grave differs from the official date of Blanche's death which is said to be 6th August. The place of the burial was possibly, at the time, quite a prized one, under a tree in the centre of the cemetery. But now the stone is in a poor condition, and leans drunkenly to one side, only standing at all because it is wedged against another. The writing is stained and faded, and it is clear the names have lost any meaning.

This was confirmed when I left a message with the church Pastor and mentioned details of the Hillyards, their achievements, their home at Bramfold, and how their grave was reportedly situated in the churchyard. The initial reaction was that I must have the wrong church, and possibly the wrong county.

So, the Hillyards may have been largely forgotten. But what is their legacy?

Let's look at Blanche first. Perhaps her legacy – the effect she has *today* on the game of tennis - is not a great one. Yet the fact remains that her achievements as a tennis player were enormous. They have been listed elsewhere and deserve recognition.

George Hillyard – what of his legacy? Like his wife he was also a strong player with achievements to his credit, although not at the same prodigious level, but is the game of tennis different today because of him? Well, the answer is, yes. Without a doubt.

The British Lawn Tennis Association must surely have been formed eventually without him, but his influence made it happen sooner. The move of the All England Club to Church Road may have happened anyway, or the new ground might have been built somewhere else, but the timeframe and detail of the build would inevitably have been different. He had influence over every aspect of it, from start to finish.

The connection of Wimbledon to the Royal Family may have grown, although it would not have happened when it did, and it would almost certainly not be as strong. In the highly conservative society of his time, the royal connection established the status of tennis, and gave it *tradition*. The relationship between Wimbledon and royalty is unique among sporting private member's clubs. Yet we take it for granted at Wimbledon and it remains part of Hillyard's legacy.

His obsession over the perfect playing conditions required for his own enjoyment spilled over into an equal and related obsession with high standards of court and conditions at Wimbledon under his stewardship. It was a bar of excellence raised high at Worple Road, and then even higher at the new ground at Church Road. The search for excellence in Wimbledon's playing conditions was another of Hillyard's legacies.

The company En-tout-cas became the largest constructor of tennis courts in the world, and remained so in Britain for three generations. It was an important company in the Leicester area, providing work at its Syston base, and beyond. Every hard tennis court at the All England Club was originally provided by En-tout-cas, and there are few major clubs in Britain which haven't at one time had courts constructed by them. Without George Hillyard the company would never have existed as a maker of tennis courts, and yet it was a part of our sporting lives for generations.

The West Sussex Golf Club would not exist without George Hillyard. He was the man who conceived the idea and obtained financial backing. Everyone who has ever played on this course or been a member of the club would not have had this pleasure but for Hillyard. Not a tennis legacy, but one of great value all the same.

Hillyard's book has proved a rich source of anecdotes and information for tennis historians. This is however, in truth, a smaller legacy than I would like. It is a real regret that he didn't write more about the game, or about his life. One of the strongest impressions I have gained from writing his biography is how quickly history fades when it moves beyond living memory. The only thing that then remains is the written word, and I am left wishing that Hillyard had written more.

Unfortunately the courts that he built on his own properties, at Thorpe Satchville and Pulborough, no longer exist. They would have been his pride and joy, lovingly created and prized as his own personal sporting stage. The greatest players of the age 'trod those boards', particularly at Thorpe Satchville. Had they survived I would just love to have been able to play a set or two at Hillyard's old home!

On the move from Worple Road to Church Road, George Hillyard evidently made a promise. '*Let us look to it that we construct and equip our ground that it will immediately be recognised as the finest, not only in England, but in the World.*'

And he succeeded. Since 1922 the grounds of the All England Club have indeed been recognised as such – the finest in England and the finest in the World. But Commander George W. Hillyard achieved too many things in too many fields to be remembered for that alone. He led a full life, from his birth in a workhouse school in Hanwell, to his end in the green fields of West Sussex; he was a man who made a difference. His life was remarkable. He was a remarkable man.

BIBLIOGRAPHY:

The following were all sources for this book, as well as fun to read.

Mostly these are books written in Hillyard's lifetime. Some can be accessed for free on the internet, others as 'Print on Demand' books, and others by buying the original. The website *www.abebooks.co.uk* is useful for giving guide prices and eBay can also be worth searching on a regular basis. And, of course, a copy of all these books can be found at the Wimbledon Library.

So, in a vague sort of personal ranking order:

Hillyard, G. W. *Forty Years of First Class Lawn Tennis*, 1924.

Myers, A. Wallis. *Lawn Tennis at Home and Abroad*, 1903.

Chipp, Herbert. *Lawn Tennis Recollections*, 1898.

Heathcote C. G. The Badminton Library of Sports and Pastimes – Lawn Tennis, 1890.

Myers, A. Wallis. *The Complete Lawn Tennis Player*, 1908.

Burrow, F. R. *My Tournaments*, 1922.

Wilding, Anthony. F. *On the Court and Off,* 1912.

Burrow, F. R. *The Centre Court and Others*, 1937.

Myers, A. Wallis. *Twenty Years of Lawn Tennis*, 1921.

Myers, A. Wallis. *Fifty Years of Wimbledon*, 1926.

Baddeley, W. *Lawn Tennis*, 1897.

Wilberforce, H. W. W. *Lawn Tennis*, 1889.

Chambers, Mrs L. *Lawn Tennis for Ladies*, 1910.

Myers, A. Wallis. *Lawn Tennis, Its Principles & Practice*, 1930.

Doherty, R. F. and H. L. *Lawn Tennis,* 1903.

Myers, A. Wallis. *Captain Anthony Wilding,* 1916.

Payn, F. W. *Tennis Topics and Tactics,* 1904.

For a more general history of lawn tennis which adequately cover Hillyard's lifespan there are two books I would recommend. The first, and best, is by Tom Todd – *The Tennis Players, from pagan rites to strawberries and cream.* This was published in 1979 in a very limited edition from his home in Jersey. If you can find a copy it may prove expensive to purchase but it's easy to read and an absolute classic.

Another tennis history is by Heiner Gillmeister – *Tennis, a cultural history.* This was published in 1997 and is very well-researched with a unique section on the history of tennis in Germany.

Wonderful resources are the early tennis periodicals: Pastime (1883-1895), Lawn Tennis Magazine (1885), Lawn Tennis (1886), Lawn Tennis and Croquet (1896-1905), Lawn Tennis and Badminton (1905-1907), Amateur Sports Illustrated (1907-1908), Lawn Tennis (1908), Lawn Tennis and Badminton (1908-1940). All are present at the Wimbledon Library.

"The Central London District Schools - a short History" is by Susan Stewart, available online.

I have read many tennis books, old and modern, and there are books I gained insight from which are not listed here. Tennis books are great – there should be a category at the Booker Prize just for them!

Bruce Tarran, Leicester 2013.